Unlocking Wealth

Unlocking Wealth

*Your Blueprint to Financial Freedom
and Prosperity*

Samuel Wealthfield

Mindful Pages

Published in 2023

ISBN: 9789357724791 (PB)
ISBN: 9789357722674 (eBook)

Published by

Mindful Pages
Imprint of Alpha Editions LLC
312 W. 2nd St #1834
Casper, WY 82601, USA

Contents

Introduction

In the realm of personal aspirations, few goals resonate as universally as the quest for financial freedom. The allure of financial independence, where one's financial situation no longer dictates life choices, beckons people from all walks of life. Whether you're a recent graduate starting your career journey, a family striving for stability, or someone seeking a newfound sense of control over their financial destiny, pursuing financial freedom is a journey worth embarking upon. This book, "Financial Freedom: Strategies for Creating Wealth and Abundance," is your guidebook for navigating this journey with confidence, wisdom, and purpose.

In today's dynamic world, financial literacy is not just a luxury; it's a necessity. Yet, despite the prevalence of financial information, many individuals grapple with questions that often lead to confusion and anxiety. What does it truly mean to be financially free? How do you escape the cycle of living paycheck to paycheck? Can you really build wealth while juggling daily expenses? These questions are the compass points guiding us as we set out to unravel the intricacies of personal finance and lay the foundation for lasting financial prosperity.

This book is designed with a singular purpose in mind: to empower you, the reader, with the knowledge, tools, and strategies needed to break free from financial limitations and embark on a journey towards abundance. Whether you're a newcomer to the world of finance or someone who's dabbled in it but seeks a deeper understanding, the chapters ahead will illuminate the path to financial freedom in a comprehensible and relatable manner.

Imagine a life where you have the freedom to make choices driven by your passions and values, rather than dictated by financial constraints. Financial freedom isn't about amassing untold riches; it's about achieving a state where your financial resources align with your life goals, granting you the liberty to focus on what truly matters. It's about having a sense of security that your financial decisions are building towards a future of limitless possibilities.

To embark on the journey towards financial freedom, one must start with a clear understanding of the financial landscape. The chapters that follow will guide you through fundamental concepts such as budgeting, saving, investing, and generating passive income. You'll learn how to create a personalized roadmap that suits your unique circumstances and aspirations. Each step will be accompanied by real-life examples, relatable stories, and practical exercises to ensure that the knowledge you acquire is not just theoretical, but actionable.

This book is a tapestry woven with diverse styles, blending the technical nuances of financial principles with the conversational tone of a trusted friend. We understand that personal finance can be overwhelming, but our aim is to simplify complex concepts without compromising on depth. By striking this balance, we hope to engage both your intellect and your intuition, making your journey towards financial freedom an enjoyable and enlightening one.

As you turn the pages of "Financial Freedom: Strategies for Creating Wealth and Abundance," remember that you hold in your hands the keys to unlock a future brimming with possibilities. Each chapter is a stepping stone towards understanding and mastery, and with every turn, you're one step closer to unraveling the mysteries of financial freedom.

Prepare to transcend the confines of financial limitations. With dedication, a thirst for knowledge, and a willingness to take action, you can rewrite your financial story and create a legacy of prosperity. The journey ahead might have its challenges, but with the right guidance and your unyielding determination, the destination of financial freedom is within reach.

So, dear reader, let us embark on this transformative expedition together. The following chapters are your map, compass, and guiding light. Welcome to "Financial Freedom: Strategies for Creating Wealth and Abundance." Your journey to a life of abundance begins now.

Importance of Financial Freedom

In a world where the pursuit of dreams often intertwines with the complexities of financial realities, the concept of financial freedom emerges as a beacon of hope and possibility. It is a term that resonates deeply across generations, transcending cultures and socioeconomic backgrounds. At its core, financial freedom is more than just a financial goal; it's a way of life that can profoundly impact one's present and future. In this article, we delve into the significance of financial freedom and how it can bring about positive, life-altering changes.

Financial freedom is a state of financial well-being where an individual's financial resources exceed their expenses, granting them the autonomy to make life choices without being hindered by financial constraints. It is not about amassing great wealth for its own sake, but rather about achieving a balance where money becomes a tool to support one's aspirations and desires.

One of the most immediate and profound impacts of financial freedom is the sense of empowerment it brings. When you have control over your finances, you regain control over your life. The constant worry about bills, debts, and unexpected expenses gradually dissipates, replaced by a feeling of security and stability. Financial freedom grants you the power to plan for the future, pursue your passions, and weather life's uncertainties without constant anxiety.

Imagine being able to pursue a career not solely for its paycheck but for the genuine interest and passion it holds. Financial freedom allows you to align your decisions with your values, rather than merely chasing financial survival. Whether it's taking a calculated career risk, embarking on a personal project, or traveling the world, the ability to make choices based on personal fulfillment rather than financial necessity is a liberating experience.

The modern world often seems like a treadmill, where individuals find themselves caught in a cycle of working to earn, only to spend their earnings on daily expenses and debt. Financial freedom offers the promise of breaking free from this cycle. With wise financial planning and disciplined saving and investing, you can gradually reduce the need for active income. This paves the way for a life where your time is truly yours, and you can pursue endeavors that resonate with your true passions.

Financial freedom not only impacts your own life but also leaves a lasting legacy for future generations. By wisely managing your resources and making thoughtful financial decisions, you can build a strong financial foundation that supports your loved ones and contributes to causes you care about. Whether it's providing for your children's education, supporting charitable initiatives, or leaving a mark on your community, financial freedom empowers you to create a positive impact that extends beyond your lifetime.

Numerous studies have highlighted the link between financial stress and overall well-being. Financial worries can lead to increased anxiety, strained relationships, and even physical health issues. Achieving financial freedom releases this burden, enabling you to focus on holistic well-being. With financial worries no longer weighing you down, you can allocate your mental and emotional energy to pursuits that nurture your mind, body, and soul.

Financial freedom is not just about the absence of financial constraints; it's about embracing a mindset of abundance. It's recognizing that there are possibilities and opportunities beyond the limitations you once perceived. This mindset shift can ripple into other areas of your life, fostering creativity, resilience, and a sense of gratitude for the resources you have.

It's important to acknowledge that the journey to financial freedom is not a one-size-fits-all endeavor. It requires careful planning, discipline, and a commitment to ongoing learning. Each individual's path will be unique, shaped by personal goals, circumstances, and timelines.

In conclusion, financial freedom is a transformative journey that goes beyond the realm of money. It is a voyage of self-discovery, empowerment, and fulfillment. By gaining control over your finances, you gain control over your life. The impact of financial freedom reaches far beyond bank accounts; it touches your relationships, your health, your dreams, and your legacy. It's an invitation to create a life that aligns with your values, passions, and aspirations—a life where you are not merely surviving, but thriving. As you embark on this journey, remember that every step you take towards financial freedom is a step towards a life of abundance and possibility.

Chapter 1: Understanding the Basics of Financial Management

Financial management, often seen as a complex puzzle, is at the heart of building a solid foundation for your financial well-being. It's not reserved for Wall Street experts; in fact, understanding the basics of financial management is crucial for everyone. Whether you're just starting your financial journey or looking to strengthen your money management skills, let's demystify the key concepts in simple terms.

Imagine your finances as a journey, and a budget as your trusty map. Budgeting is the art of tracking your income and expenses, helping you allocate your money wisely. Begin by listing your sources of income—your paycheck, side hustles, or any other earnings. Next, list your expenses—rent, utilities, groceries, entertainment, and so on. The goal is to ensure that your expenses don't exceed your income. This map guides you, preventing overspending and helping you save for future goals.

Saving money is like planting seeds for a rainy day. It's a cushion that ensures you're prepared for unexpected expenses or emergencies. Start with an emergency fund—a stash of cash equivalent to a few months' worth of living expenses. This fund acts as a safety net, providing peace of mind when the unexpected occurs. Once your emergency fund is established, you can focus on saving for specific goals like buying a car, going on a vacation, or even investing.

Imagine your money growing on its own, like a tree that bears fruit year after year. That's the power of compound interest. It's the interest you earn not only on your initial investment but also on the interest that accumulates over time. The earlier you start saving, the more time your money has to grow. This means even small contributions can lead to significant growth thanks to compounding.

Not all debt is bad, but it requires careful handling. Good debt, like a student loan or a mortgage, can help you build a better future. Bad debt, like high-interest credit card debt, can be a trap that hinders your financial progress. Aim to pay off high-interest debt as soon as possible while managing lower-interest debt responsibly.

Think of your credit score as a report card for your financial behavior. It's a number that summarizes your creditworthiness and determines your ability to secure loans and better interest rates. Paying bills on time, keeping credit card balances low, and avoiding unnecessary debt can help maintain a healthy credit score.

Investing is like planting seeds in a garden that yields fruits over time. It involves putting your money into various assets—stocks, bonds, real estate, and more—with the aim of growing your wealth. Investing requires understanding risk and rewards, and it's best approached with a long-term perspective. Starting small and gradually increasing your investments can help you navigate this terrain.

Think of your financial goals as destinations on your journey. Whether it's buying a home, paying off debt, saving for retirement, or funding your child's education, setting clear financial goals gives your journey purpose. Goals keep you motivated and help you make informed financial decisions aligned with your aspirations.

Understanding the basics of financial management is like laying the groundwork for a sturdy house. It's about creating a strong financial foundation supporting your dreams and shielding you from financial shocks. You're taking control of your financial future by budgeting wisely, saving diligently, managing debt responsibly, and making informed investment decisions. Remember, financial management is a journey, not a race. It's okay to start small and learn along the way. With determination, knowledge, and a commitment to your financial well-being, you'll find yourself well-prepared to tackle any financial challenge that comes your way. Your journey towards financial empowerment begins now.

Demystifying Financial Jargon: A Guide to Key Concepts

Entering the world of personal finance can sometimes feel like navigating a foreign land filled with unfamiliar terms and concepts. But fear not! Just as every journey begins with a single step, every financial journey begins with understanding the basics. Let's break down some key financial terms and concepts to provide you with a sturdy foundation for your financial exploration.

1. Assets and Liabilities:

Assets: These are things you own that hold value, such as money in your bank account, your home, investments, and even your car. Assets contribute to your net worth.

Liabilities: These are your financial obligations or debts, such as credit card balances, student loans, and mortgages. Liabilities subtract from your net worth.

2. Net Worth:

Your net worth is a snapshot of your financial health. It's calculated by subtracting your total liabilities from your total assets. A positive net worth means your assets exceed your debts, while a negative net worth indicates the opposite.

3. Income and Expenses:

Income: This is the money you earn, whether from a job, investments, or other sources.

Expenses: These are your financial outflows, including bills, groceries, entertainment, and more. Tracking expenses helps you understand where your money is going.

4. Budget:

A budget is a plan that outlines your expected income and expenses over a period of time. It helps you manage your money, allocate funds to different categories, and ensure you're living within your means.

5. Savings:

Savings refer to the money you set aside for future needs or goals. It acts as a safety net and can also be used for investments or larger purchases.

6. Compound Interest:

Compound interest is the interest earned on both the initial amount of money (principal) and the interest that has accumulated over time. It leads to exponential growth of your investments over the long term.

7. Credit Score:

A credit score is a numerical representation of your creditworthiness. Lenders use it to assess your ability to repay loans. A higher credit score typically leads to better loan terms.

8. Investment:

Investing involves putting your money into assets like stocks, bonds, or real estate with the goal of growing your wealth over time. Investments come with risks and potential rewards.

9. Debt and Credit:

Debt: Debt is money you owe to creditors, such as loans or credit card balances.

Credit: Credit refers to your ability to borrow money based on your promise to repay. Credit cards and loans are common examples.

10. Financial Goals:

Financial goals are specific objectives you set for your financial future. They can include saving for retirement, buying a home, paying off debt, or funding education.

11. Emergency Fund:

An emergency fund is a savings cushion set aside for unexpected expenses, like medical bills or car repairs. It provides financial security and prevents the need to go into debt for unforeseen situations.

12. Retirement Planning:

Retirement planning involves saving and investing for your retirement years. Retirement accounts, like 401(k)s and IRAs, help you accumulate funds to support your lifestyle after you stop working.

Understanding these foundational terms and concepts is akin to learning the language of personal finance. Armed with this knowledge, you'll have a clearer understanding of financial discussions, make informed decisions, and lay the groundwork for a prosperous financial future. As you delve deeper into your financial journey, remember that everyone starts somewhere, and your willingness to learn and grow will propel you toward greater financial literacy and success.

The Significance of Setting Goals and Creating a Roadmap

Picture yourself embarking on a cross-country road trip without a map or destination. Chances are, you'd end up lost, wasting time, and feeling frustrated. Just as a roadmap guides you on a journey, setting financial goals and creating a roadmap for your finances is crucial for steering your financial journey in the right direction. In this article, we explore the importance of setting financial goals and how they serve as the compass to guide you towards a prosperous future.

1. Providing Direction and Purpose:

Imagine sailing a ship without a destination. You'd be adrift, tossed around by currents and winds. Similarly, financial goals give your money a purpose and a direction. They provide you with a clear destination to work towards. Whether buying a home, starting a business, or retiring comfortably, financial goals give your financial decisions a sense of purpose.

2. Motivation and Focus:

Having concrete financial goals keeps you motivated and focused. When you can visualise the rewards that achieving your goals will bring, you're more likely to stay disciplined in your financial decisions. Goals give you something to look forward to and a reason to save and invest.

3. Prioritizing Spending and Saving:

Financial goals act as filters for your spending decisions. When you have a clear goal in mind, you're more likely to differentiate between wants and needs. This helps you allocate your resources wisely, ensuring your money is directed towards achieving what truly matters to you.

4. Measuring Progress:

Imagine driving without road signs. You wouldn't know how far you've come or how far you have left to go. Financial goals provide you with milestones to track your progress. Regularly assessing your progress keeps you accountable and allows you to make necessary adjustments.

5. Building a Strategy:

A roadmap isn't just about the destination; it's about the route you take to get there. Similarly, financial goals require a plan of action. Creating a roadmap involves breaking down your big goals into smaller, manageable steps. This strategy helps you chart a course that guides you toward your ultimate objective.

6. Adapting to Changes:

Life is filled with unexpected twists and turns. Just as a GPS recalculates your route when you take a detour, having a financial roadmap allows you to adapt to changes. Whether it's a job loss, a medical emergency, or a new opportunity, your financial roadmap can help you make informed decisions without losing sight of your goals.

7. Building Discipline and Habit:

Setting and working towards financial goals instills discipline and healthy financial habits. It encourages you to save consistently, budget responsibly, and make mindful spending choices. Over time, these behaviors become second nature, contributing to your overall financial well-being.

8. Celebrating Achievements:

Reaching a destination after a long journey is immensely satisfying. The same applies to financial goals. When you achieve a financial milestone, it's important to celebrate your achievements. Recognizing your progress boosts your confidence and motivates you to continue working towards bigger goals.

9. Creating Financial Confidence:

Financial goals provide a sense of control over your financial future. They empower you to take charge of your money and make informed decisions. As you achieve your goals, you'll gain confidence in your financial abilities, fostering a positive relationship with money.

10. Crafting Your Financial Story:

Ultimately, setting financial goals is about taking ownership of your financial narrative. It's about creating a story where you're in control, making purposeful decisions that align with your values and aspirations. By setting goals and crafting a roadmap, you're actively shaping your financial destiny.

Just as a roadmap ensures a successful journey, financial goals provide direction and purpose to your financial journey. They guide you through the twists and turns of life, helping you make informed decisions and stay focused on what matters most. By setting clear goals and creating a roadmap, you're not just managing money; you're steering your life towards a destination of financial well-being and prosperity. Your journey begins with setting your first goal and taking that decisive step towards a brighter financial future.

Chapter 2: Building a Strong Financial Foundation through Budgeting

In the bustling landscape of personal finance, where every dollar earned has the potential to shape your financial destiny, lies the cornerstone of financial well-being: budgeting. This chapter delves deep into the art and science of budgeting—a practice that has the power to transform your financial present and future.

Understanding the Budgeting Landscape

Imagine constructing a grand skyscraper without a solid foundation. The result would be instability and uncertainty. Similarly, your financial life needs a robust foundation to support your aspirations and dreams. Budgeting, often misconstrued as restrictive, is the scaffolding that strengthens this foundation. It systematically allocates your income towards various needs, wants, and goals, ensuring that you live within your means while striving towards financial growth.

The Purpose of Budgeting

At its core, budgeting is not about deprivation; it's about empowerment. It empowers you to allocate your resources strategically, putting you in control of your finances rather than being controlled by them. With a well-structured budget, you're equipped to:

1. Set Clear Financial Goals:

Budgeting serves as the blueprint for your financial journey. It helps you set realistic goals—whether it's paying off debt, saving for a vacation, or building an emergency fund. By giving every dollar a purpose, you're directing your financial efforts towards your dreams.

2. Manage Income and Expenses:

Just as a captain navigates a ship through turbulent waters, a budget helps you steer through financial challenges. It provides clarity on your inflows and outflows, allowing you to adjust your spending habits as needed. This adaptability is essential for staying on course even in unpredictable financial circumstances.

3. Prioritize Spending:

Budgeting acts as a filter in a world brimming with choices and temptations. It helps you distinguish between needs and wants, covering essential expenses before discretionary spending. This ensures that you're consistently working towards your goals without succumbing to impulsive spending.

4. Eliminate Financial Stress:

Picture a life where you're free from the constant worry of unpaid bills and mounting debt. Budgeting creates financial predictability, reducing stress and enhancing your overall well-being. When you know exactly where your money is going, you gain peace of mind.

5. Increase Savings and Investments:

Budgeting is your tool for building a brighter financial future. By allocating a portion of your income to savings and investments, you're cultivating a habit of financial growth. As you accumulate funds, you're better prepared for opportunities and challenges that come your way.

6. Promote Financial Communication:

Budgeting isn't just an individual endeavor; it's a collaborative practice. Couples and families benefit greatly from budgeting as it encourages open discussions about financial goals, priorities, and strategies. It fosters financial unity and helps everyone align their efforts.

7. Achieve Financial Freedom:

At its pinnacle, budgeting leads to financial freedom. By managing your resources wisely, you're building a stable platform from which you can pursue your dreams and desires. Financial freedom is about living life on your terms, unburdened by financial constraints.

The Art of Creating a Budget

Creating a budget is akin to crafting a work of art—a masterpiece that combines creativity, strategy, and practicality. It's not a one-size-fits-all endeavor; rather, it's a personalized plan that reflects your unique financial landscape. Here's a glimpse into the steps that form the canvas of a well-structured budget:

1. Assess Your Finances:

Begin by understanding your current financial situation. Calculate your total income and list all your expenses. This gives you a clear picture of where your money is currently going.

2. Set Clear Goals:

Identify your short-term and long-term financial goals. These can range from paying off credit card debt to saving for a down payment on a home. Goals provide the motivation and direction needed for budgeting success.

3. Categorize Your Expenses:

Divide your expenses into categories such as housing, transportation, groceries, entertainment, and savings. This segmentation allows you to see where your money is being spent and identify areas for potential adjustments.

4. Allocate Funds:

Distribute your income across the various expense categories based on priority. Essentials like housing and utilities take precedence, followed by discretionary spending. Don't forget to allocate funds for savings and investments.

5. Monitor and Adjust:

Creating a budget is just the beginning; maintaining it requires consistent effort. Regularly track your spending and compare it to your budgeted amounts. If you notice discrepancies, make necessary adjustments to stay on track.

6. Embrace Flexibility:

Life is dynamic, and your budget should reflect that. Be prepared to adapt your budget based on changing circumstances, such as income fluctuations or unexpected expenses.

7. Celebrate Milestones:

As you adhere to your budget and achieve your financial milestones, celebrate your successes. Recognizing your progress strengthens your commitment to your financial goals.

A Step-by-Step Guide to Budgeting and Expense Tracking

As we delve deeper into this pivotal topic, let's break down the budgeting process step by step, unraveling the art of tracking expenses and creating a budget that aligns with your financial aspirations.

Step 1: Track Your Expenses

Imagine a treasure map with marked waypoints. Tracking expenses is your way of marking every financial waypoint on your journey. This step unveils where your money goes, shedding light on patterns and habits that can influence your financial decisions.

a. Gather Your Financial Information:

Collect all your financial documents—bank statements, credit card bills, receipts, and invoices. A comprehensive financial transaction overview forms the foundation for accurate expense tracking.

b. Categorize Your Expenses:

Sort your expenses into categories such as housing, transportation, groceries, entertainment, utilities, and more. This categorization helps you understand your spending habits and identify areas where you may need to make adjustments.

c. Use Technology to Your Advantage:

Leverage financial tracking apps or spreadsheet tools to streamline the process. These tools automatically categorize transactions and provide visual representations of your spending patterns.

d. Set a Time Frame:

Choose a specific time frame—such as a month—to track your expenses. This snapshot gives you a comprehensive view of your spending habits over a defined period.

e. Be Thorough and Honest:

Honesty is the key to accurate expense tracking. Record every expense, no matter how small. Even seemingly insignificant expenses can add up over time.

Step 2: Creating Your Budget

With a detailed understanding of your spending patterns, you're ready to construct your budget—a roadmap that guides your financial choices and aspirations.

a. Determine Your Income:

List all sources of income, including your salary, side gigs, investments, and any other earnings. This provides a clear picture of the funds available for budgeting.

b. Identify Fixed Expenses:

Fixed expenses are recurring costs that remain relatively stable from month to month. These include rent or mortgage payments, utility bills, loan payments, and insurance premiums.

c. Allocate Variable Expenses:

Variable expenses are flexible and can change from month to month. These include groceries, entertainment, dining out, and discretionary spending. Use insights from your expense tracking to set reasonable limits for each category.

d. Set Financial Goals:

Allocate funds for your financial goals, whether it's building an emergency fund, paying off debt, saving for a vacation, or investing. Prioritize these goals based on their importance to your overall financial well-being.

e. Create a Surplus:

The goal of budgeting isn't just to break even—it's to create a surplus. Allocate funds for savings and investments to grow your wealth over time. Even a small surplus can lead to significant financial growth through the magic of compound interest.

f. Review and Adjust:

Your budget is a living document that requires periodic review and adjustment. Revisit your budget regularly to ensure that it accurately reflects your financial situation and goals. If you find that certain categories consistently exceed their limits, consider making adjustments to avoid overspending.

Step 3: Crafting a Realistic Budget

With a clear understanding of your income, expenses, and financial goals, you're ready to craft a budget that reflects your financial reality and aspirations.

a. Begin with Your Income:

Your income is the canvas upon which your budget is painted. List all sources of income, ensuring that you include both regular paychecks and any additional income streams. This gives you a comprehensive view of the funds available for allocation.

b. Break Down Fixed Expenses:

Fixed expenses, such as rent or mortgage payments, utility bills, and loan payments, remain consistent from month to month. List these expenses along with their respective amounts. This provides a baseline for your essential financial commitments.

c. Tackle Variable Expenses:

Variable expenses, which include categories like groceries, entertainment, and discretionary spending, require a closer look. Refer to the insights gained from tracking your expenses to set reasonable limits for each category. Be mindful of areas where you can cut back without sacrificing your quality of life.

d. Allocate for Savings and Investments:

Allocate a portion of your income towards savings and investments. These funds are the seeds for your financial future, allowing you to build an emergency fund, pay off debt, and invest for growth. The earlier you start saving, the more time your money has to compound and grow.

e. Consider Financial Goals:

Your budget should reflect your financial goals and aspirations. Allocate funds specifically for achieving these goals, whether it's funding a vacation, starting a business, or buying a home. By earmarking funds for your goals, you're making intentional progress towards realizing your dreams.

Step 4: Review and Adjust Regularly

Creating a budget isn't a one-time activity; it's an ongoing process that requires attention and adjustment. Regular review ensures that your budget remains aligned with your financial circumstances and goals.

a. Monthly Check-ins:

Set aside time each month to review your budget and compare it to your actual spending. This helps you identify any discrepancies or areas where you overspent. Adjust your budget as needed to ensure that your spending aligns with your allocations.

b. Accommodate Changes:

Life is full of changes—some expected, some not. As you encounter life events such as job changes, salary adjustments, or unexpected expenses, be prepared to adapt your budget accordingly. Flexibility is key to ensuring your budget remains relevant.

c. Celebrate Milestones:

As you adhere to your budget and make progress towards your financial goals, celebrate your achievements. Each milestone reached is a testament to your dedication and discipline. Recognizing these achievements boosts your motivation to continue on your financial journey.

d. Seek Continuous Improvement:

Your budget is a tool for constant refinement. Over time, you'll develop a keen understanding of your spending habits, allowing you to make more informed financial decisions. Strive to continually refine your budget to better align with your evolving goals and aspirations.

The Art of Empowerment

Budgeting is more than just tracking numbers; it's a practice that empowers you to take control of your financial journey. By tracking your expenses and creating a budget, you're equipping yourself with the tools to make informed financial decisions. You're shifting from being a passive observer of your finances to an active participant in shaping your financial future.

Every dollar you earn has the potential to contribute to your goals, dreams, and aspirations. Budgeting ensures that your hard-earned money is aligned with your values and priorities. It provides the framework for financial discipline, growth, and ultimately, freedom.

Crafting a budget is not just a financial exercise; it's a journey of self-awareness and empowerment. It's about understanding your relationship with money, prioritizing your values, and making choices that resonate with your aspirations. By tracking your expenses and creating a budget, you're engaging in an artful practice that guides you towards financial success and abundance.

Your budget is your compass, helping you navigate the complex landscape of personal finance. It's a tool that empowers you to achieve your goals, make mindful spending decisions, and build a strong financial foundation. As you embrace the art of budgeting, remember that every dollar you allocate has the potential to shape your financial destiny. By taking charge of your finances today, you're sculpting a future of prosperity and freedom.

Chapter 3: Unlocking Financial Growth: The Journey of Saving and Compound Interest

In the world of personal finance, two seemingly unassuming concepts can transform your financial journey into a tale of abundance and prosperity. At the heart of every financial success story lies a simple yet profound practice: saving. Saving isn't just about stashing away money; it's about creating a foundation that supports your goals, empowers your decisions, and nurtures your dreams. It's the cornerstone of financial stability, enabling you to weather storms, seize opportunities, and achieve milestones that shape your future.

But the magic doesn't stop at saving alone. Enter the scene: compound interest—a force so powerful that even Albert Einstein referred to it as the "eighth wonder of the world." Compound interest is the secret ingredient that transforms your saved dollars into an engine of exponential growth. It's the catalyst that propels your financial endeavors to new heights, turning small contributions into substantial sums over time.

Consider this: as you set aside money and let it accumulate, it not only grows based on the interest you earn but also on the interest that you've previously earned. This compounding effect creates a snowball effect, causing your savings to grow at an accelerating rate. It's a virtuous cycle where your money starts working for you, and the more time you give it, the more it multiplies.

The beauty of compound interest lies in its patience. It rewards those who start early and consistently contribute, allowing time to magnify the impact. Even modest contributions, when given enough time, can blossom into substantial wealth. The secret isn't just about how much you save, but about how early you begin and how consistently you contribute.

Imagine starting a journey with a single step, and with each subsequent step, your stride becomes longer and more powerful. That's the essence of compound interest—an incremental growth that gains momentum as it progresses. It's a testament to the value of patience, discipline, and a long-term perspective in the world of finance.

Together, saving and compound interest form a synergy that empowers your financial journey. They're not just concepts; they're the architects of your wealth, shaping the landscape of your future. They're the allies that enable you to achieve your dreams, whether it's buying a home, funding your child's education, or retiring comfortably.

The power of saving and compound interest is universal—it transcends age, income, and background. Whether you're just starting your career, raising a family, or planning for retirement, their principles remain relevant and impactful. They're the tools that level the playing field, allowing you to take control of your financial destiny.

As we delve deeper into this chapter, we'll uncover the mechanics of compound interest and explore strategies to optimize your saving efforts. We'll discuss the significance of starting early and staying consistent and the various avenues through which you can harness the power of compounding. Moreover, we'll highlight real-life success stories that exemplify the potential of this dynamic duo.

So, fasten your seatbelt as we journey through the realms of saving and compound interest. Get ready to unlock the full potential of your financial resources and witness the extraordinary growth that awaits you. Whether you're a novice in the world of finance or a seasoned investor, the principles we'll explore in this chapter have the capacity to redefine your financial trajectory.

The journey ahead is one of empowerment, enlightenment, and enrichment. It's a journey that invites you to master the art of saving, embrace the magic of compound interest, and chart a course towards financial freedom. As we embark on this voyage, remember that every dollar you save and every day you allow for compounding is a step towards shaping your financial destiny. The future is yours to mold, and the power of saving and compound interest is your guiding light towards a realm of boundless wealth and abundance.

The Transformative Power of Saving Money

In the quest for financial freedom and abundance, few practices wield as much influence as the simple yet profound act of saving money. Saving is more than just setting aside a portion of your income; it's a strategic decision that empowers you to take control of your financial journey and craft a future of security, opportunities, and dreams fulfilled. In this exploration of the significance of saving money, we delve into why saving matters, how it can be accomplished, and the pivotal role it plays in paving the way to financial freedom.

Why Saving Matters:

Saving money isn't merely about accumulating wealth; it's about fostering financial resilience, aligning your actions with your goals, and creating a buffer against life's uncertainties. Here's a closer look at why saving is paramount on your path to financial freedom:

1. Creating a Safety Net: Life is unpredictable, and unexpected expenses can arise at any moment—a medical emergency, car repair, or sudden job loss. Building an emergency fund cushions you against such shocks, enabling you to navigate these challenges without derailing your long-term financial plans.

2. Seizing Opportunities: Opportunities don't always knock twice. Whether it's investing in a promising venture, pursuing further education, or capitalizing on a market shift, having savings at your disposal empowers you to grasp these chances without incurring debt or compromising your financial stability.

3. Breaking the Debt Cycle: High-interest debt can be a relentless cycle that drains your resources and shackles your financial growth. By saving and having funds to cover expenses, you reduce the need to rely on credit cards or loans for everyday needs, thus breaking free from the cycle of debt.

4. Enabling Financial Autonomy: Saving fosters financial independence—a state where your choices are governed by your values and aspirations, not by external constraints. Having savings provides you with the freedom to make decisions based on what's important to you, rather than being limited by financial constraints.

5. Building Wealth Over Time: Saving is the cornerstone of wealth creation. Over time, even small, consistent contributions can accumulate and grow substantially due to the power of compound interest. Your savings become the seeds from which a forest of financial abundance can sprout.

How to Save Effectively:

While the importance of saving is clear, the "how" can often be a challenge. Here are practical strategies to help you embark on your saving journey:

1. Set Clear Goals: Define your financial goals—short-term, mid-term, and long-term. Whether it's buying a home, starting a business, or retiring comfortably, having specific goals gives your savings purpose and direction.

2. Create a Budget: A budget is your financial roadmap. List your income, categorize your expenses, and allocate a portion for savings. Treat savings as a non-negotiable expense, just like paying bills, to ensure consistent contributions.

3. Pay Yourself First: Adopt the practice of paying yourself first by automating your savings. Set up automatic transfers from your main account to a dedicated savings or investment account. This eliminates the temptation to spend before saving.

4. Start Small and Gradually Increase: If saving seems daunting, begin with a modest amount and gradually increase it over time. The key is consistency. Even small contributions can have a significant impact when compounded over the years.

5. Reduce Discretionary Spending: Identify areas where you can cut back on discretionary spending. Review your expenses and look for opportunities to save without sacrificing your quality of life. Redirect these funds towards your savings goals.

6. Minimize Lifestyle Inflation: As your income increases, avoid succumbing to lifestyle inflation—where your expenses rise in tandem with your income. Instead, direct the additional income towards savings and investments.

7. Avoid Impulse Purchases: Practice mindful spending by resisting impulsive purchases. Before making a non-essential purchase, give yourself a cooling-off period to determine if it aligns with your priorities.

8. Track Your Progress: Regularly monitor your savings progress and celebrate milestones achieved. Tracking your growth reinforces positive behavior and motivates you to stay on course.

The Role of Saving in Achieving Financial Freedom:

As you embark on your journey towards financial freedom, recognize that saving is the cornerstone upon which your dreams are built. It's the manifestation of your commitment to yourself and your future. Here's how saving money plays a pivotal role in the pursuit of financial freedom:

1. Cultivating Discipline: Saving cultivates financial discipline. It requires you to make intentional choices, prioritize your needs over wants, and consistently allocate funds towards your goals. This discipline spills over into other areas of your financial life, contributing to your overall success.

2. Harnessing Compound Interest: Saving money is the catalyst that unleashes the magic of compound interest. As you save and invest, your money generates returns that, in turn, generate more returns. Over time, this compounding effect accelerates the growth of your wealth, allowing your savings to work tirelessly on your behalf.

3. Building a Strong Foundation: Financial freedom requires a solid foundation, and saving is the bedrock upon which that foundation is laid. It provides you with the resources to weather storms, pursue opportunities, and make choices aligned with your values.

4. Redefining Financial Choices: As your savings grow, your financial choices expand. You gain the freedom to make decisions that align with your aspirations rather than being constrained by financial limitations. This empowerment redefines your relationship with money and the possibilities it presents.

5. Achieving Milestones: Saving money propels you towards achieving financial milestones. Whether it's paying off debt, buying a home, or retiring comfortably, your savings form the bridge that connects your current reality to your desired future.

6. Creating Peace of Mind: Financial freedom is not just about wealth; it's also about peace of mind. Having savings grants you the security and tranquility to face life's challenges without the anxiety of financial strain. It empowers you to focus on living your life fully.

7. Fostering Generational Wealth: Saving isn't just for your benefit; it's a legacy you can pass on to future generations. By building a strong financial foundation, you're setting the stage for generational wealth that can positively impact your family's future.

Saving money isn't a mere financial exercise; it's a lifestyle that reflects your commitment to a future of freedom and abundance. By embracing the significance of saving and integrating it into your financial strategy, you're taking control of your financial narrative. You're making a conscious choice to prioritize your dreams, strengthen your resilience, and harness the transformative power of compound interest.

As you journey towards financial freedom, remember that every dollar you save is an investment in your future. It's a declaration of your intention to shape your destiny, achieve your aspirations, and experience a life unrestrained by financial limitations. Your savings are the seeds from which prosperity grows—a testament to your dedication, discipline, and unwavering belief in the boundless possibilities that lie ahead.

Understanding Compound Interest and Its Transformative Power

In the realm of personal finance, few concepts possess the mesmerizing allure and potential for exponential growth quite like compound interest. Often referred to as the "magic of compounding," this phenomenon is not merely a financial principle; it's a force that has the power to turn modest savings into substantial wealth over time. In this exploration of compound interest, we unravel the mystery behind its workings, its role in growing savings, and the various avenues through which you can harness its enchanting potential.

The Essence of Compound Interest:

At its core, compound interest is interest calculated on both the initial sum of money and the accumulated interest that has been previously added. In simpler terms, it's interest that earns interest. This dynamic creates a ripple effect, causing your savings to grow at an accelerating rate as time progresses. The key to unlocking the full potential of compound interest lies in patience and consistency.

The Mechanics of Growth:

Imagine planting a seed in fertile soil. Over time, that seed germinates, sprouts, and eventually becomes a towering tree with fruit. Compound interest operates on a similar principle, but instead of soil, it's fueled by financial contributions and the passage of time.

Here's how it works: when you invest or save money, you earn a return on your initial investment. In subsequent periods, you earn interest not only on the initial amount but also on the previously earned interest. This compounding effect causes your money to grow more rapidly, as each interest payment contributes to the next growth cycle.

The Role of Time and Consistency:

The true magic of compound interest lies in the relationship between time and consistency. The longer your money is allowed to compound, the more dramatic the growth becomes. Even modest contributions, given enough time, can lead to substantial wealth accumulation.

To illustrate this, consider two scenarios: Investor A starts saving $1,000 per year at age 25 and stops at age 35, while Investor B starts saving the same amount at age 35 and continues until age 65. Despite contributing the same amount, Investor A benefits from a more extended compounding period, resulting in significantly greater wealth by age 65.

Investment Avenues for Harnessing Compound Interest:

Now that we've demystified the mechanics of compound interest, let's explore the various investment avenues that enable you to capitalize on its growth potential:

1. Savings Accounts: While traditional savings accounts offer relatively low interest rates, they're a secure and easily accessible option for keeping your emergency fund or short-term savings. Although the growth might be gradual, every dollar you save earns a bit more over time.

2. Certificates of Deposit (CDs): CDs are time-bound investments where you agree to keep your money deposited for a fixed period. In return, you receive a higher interest rate than a regular savings account. They're particularly suitable for conservative investors looking for a predictable return.

3. Bonds: Bonds are debt securities issued by governments or corporations. When you buy a bond, you're essentially lending money in exchange for regular interest payments (coupon) and the return of the principal amount upon maturity. Bonds provide a reliable stream of income with the potential for capital appreciation.

4. Stocks and Dividends: Investing in stocks offers the opportunity for capital appreciation, and many companies pay dividends—a portion of their profits—to shareholders. By reinvesting these dividends, you're harnessing the power of compound interest, as your dividend earnings generate additional returns over time.

5. Mutual Funds and Exchange-Traded Funds (ETFs): Mutual funds and ETFs pool money from multiple investors to invest in a diversified portfolio of assets. By investing in these funds, you gain exposure to a variety of investments, potentially benefiting from the compounded growth of the underlying assets.

6. Retirement Accounts: Retirement accounts, such as Individual Retirement Accounts (IRAs) and 401(k)s, offer tax advantages that amplify the impact of compound interest. Contributions grow tax-deferred, allowing your investments to compound without the drag of immediate taxes.

7. Real Estate Investments: Real estate investments, such as rental properties, can generate rental income and appreciate in value over time. This dual benefit creates a fertile ground for compound interest, as your property generates returns on both the rent and potential appreciation.

8. Compound Interest Accounts: Certain financial institutions offer specialized compound interest accounts designed to maximize the growth potential of your savings. These accounts often come with higher interest rates and favourable terms to encourage long-term saving.

9. Peer-to-Peer Lending: Peer-to-peer lending platforms allow individuals to lend money directly to borrowers, earning interest on their investments. While this comes with a degree of risk, it presents an alternative way to generate compound interest.

10. Retirement Annuities: Retirement annuities are insurance contracts that provide regular payments during retirement. Annuities offer various options, such as fixed, variable, or indexed annuities, each with its own approach to generating interest and potential growth.

The concept of compound interest is not just a mathematical abstraction; it's a guiding principle that has the power to shape your financial future. By understanding its mechanics and exploring diverse investment avenues, you're equipped to harness its transformative potential. As you embark on your journey towards financial growth, remember that every contribution you make, every investment you choose, and every day you allow for compounding is a step towards cultivating a future of prosperity, abundance, and the realization of your financial aspirations. The magic of compound interest is your ally—a steadfast companion on the path to a life unrestrained by financial limitations.

Chapter 4: Getting Started with Smart Investing

Investing is like planting a seed for a future financial harvest. Whether you're looking to build wealth, achieve financial goals, or secure your retirement, smart investing can be your trusty companion on the journey to financial success. In this article, we'll explore the fundamental principles of getting started with smart investing, demystifying the process and empowering you to make informed choices.

Understanding the Why: Setting Your Investment Goals

Before diving into the world of investments, defining your objectives is crucial. What are you investing for? Your goals will shape your investment strategy and guide your decision-making. Common investment goals include:

Wealth Building: Accumulating assets and growing your net worth over time.

Retirement Planning: Ensuring a comfortable and financially secure retirement.

Education Funding: Saving for your children's education expenses.

Homeownership: Saving for a down payment on a home.

Emergency Fund: Building a financial safety net for unexpected expenses.

Short-Term Goals: Investing for near-future expenses, like a vacation or a new car.

Knowing your goals will help you determine your investment horizon, risk tolerance, and the types of investments that align with your objectives.

The Investment Pyramid: Building a Solid Foundation

Imagine your investment portfolio as a pyramid, with different layers representing various asset classes and investment types. At the base of the pyramid are low-risk, stable investments, while riskier, potentially higher-reward investments occupy the upper layers. Here's a breakdown of the investment pyramid:

> **Foundation (Base):** The foundation consists of safe, liquid investments like savings accounts, certificates of deposit (CDs), and money market funds. These provide stability and easy access to cash, making them ideal for emergency funds and short-term goals.
>
> **Income (Second Layer):** Income-producing assets like bonds, dividend-paying stocks, and real estate investment trusts (REITs) are above the foundation. These investments offer a steady income stream while maintaining a moderate level of risk.
>
> **Growth (Third Layer):** The growth layer includes growth-oriented assets like individual stocks, exchange-traded funds (ETFs), and mutual funds. These investments have the potential for capital appreciation but come with higher volatility.
>
> **Speculation (Top):** At the top of the pyramid are speculative investments, such as individual stocks in emerging industries or high-risk ventures. These carry the potential for significant gains but also heightened risk.

Your investment pyramid should reflect your risk tolerance and investment horizon. It's essential to have a diversified portfolio that combines elements from each layer to manage risk and achieve your financial goals.

The Golden Rule: Diversification

Diversification is the cornerstone of smart investing. It involves spreading your investments across different asset classes and types to reduce risk. The rationale behind diversification is simple: when one investment underperforms, others may offset the losses, preserving your overall portfolio value.

Types of Investments:

> **Stocks:** Owning shares of a company's stock means you own a piece of that company. Stocks offer the potential for high returns but come with greater volatility.

> **Bonds:** Bonds are debt securities issued by governments or corporations. When you buy a bond, you're essentially lending money in exchange for regular interest payments (coupon) and the return of the principal amount upon maturity.

> **Mutual Funds:** Mutual funds pool money from multiple investors to invest in a diversified portfolio of stocks, bonds, or other assets. They provide instant diversification and professional management.

> **Exchange-Traded Funds (ETFs):** Similar to mutual funds, ETFs track an index or a basket of assets. They trade on stock exchanges, offering liquidity and diversification.

> **Real Estate:** Investing in real estate can involve purchasing physical properties or investing in real estate investment trusts (REITs), which provide exposure to the real estate market without the need for direct property ownership.

> Commodities include physical goods like gold, oil, and agricultural products. Investing in commodities can act as a hedge against inflation and diversify your portfolio.

Risk Management: Assessing Your Tolerance

Understanding your risk tolerance is paramount in making smart investment decisions. Risk tolerance is your ability and willingness to withstand fluctuations in the value of your investments. It's influenced by factors like your financial goals, investment horizon, and psychological comfort with market volatility.

Assessing your risk tolerance involves asking yourself questions like:

> How comfortable am I with the idea of losing some of my invested capital?

> What is my investment horizon? (Short-term, medium-term, long-term)

> Can I emotionally handle the ups and downs of the stock market?

> Am I financially prepared for unexpected emergencies or expenses?

Your risk tolerance will help you determine the mix of assets in your portfolio and the proportion of each asset class.

Time is Your Ally: The Power of Compounding

The sooner you start investing, the more time your money has to grow through the power of compound interest. Compound interest is the concept of earning interest on both your initial investment and the accumulated interest from previous periods. It's like a snowball effect, where your investments grow exponentially over time.

Even though both individuals invest the same amount, Person A, who started earlier, will likely accumulate more wealth due to the longer time for compound interest to work its magic.

Stay Informed: Continuous Learning

Investing is not a one-time activity; it's an ongoing process. Markets change, economic conditions evolve, and investment opportunities arise. Staying informed is crucial for making informed decisions.

> **Read Financial News:** Keep up with financial news and market updates to understand current trends and events that may impact your investments.

Educate Yourself: Invest in your financial education. Books, courses, and online resources are valuable tools for enhancing your knowledge.

Consult Professionals: Consider working with financial advisors or investment professionals who can provide expert guidance tailored to your goals.

Patience and Discipline: The Keys to Success

Successful investing requires patience and discipline. Avoid the temptation to react impulsively to market fluctuations or chase short-term gains. Stick to your investment plan, stay focused on your goals, and remember that investing is a long-term journey.

In conclusion, starting with intelligent investing is crucial to achieving your financial goals. By defining your objectives, diversifying your portfolio, assessing your risk tolerance, harnessing the power of compounding, staying informed, and maintaining discipline, you can confidently navigate the world of investments. Smart investing is not just about making money; it's about securing your financial future and empowering yourself to achieve your dreams.

Demystifying Stocks, Bonds, and Mutual Funds

The world of investing is a realm filled with opportunities, risks, and a diverse array of financial instruments. It's a landscape where fortunes are made, and where prudent decisions can pave the way to financial freedom. Yet, for the uninitiated, the jargon and complexity of investing can be daunting. In this exploration, we shall be your guides into this realm, demystifying key terms like stocks, bonds, and mutual funds and illuminating the path to making informed investment choices.

Investing: A Voyage of Financial Growth

Investing is the act of deploying your money with the expectation of generating returns or profits in the future. It's the process of setting your money to work like a partner in a grand financial endeavor. The goal? To make your money grow and fulfill financial aspirations, whether that be securing retirement, funding a child's education, or simply building wealth.

Stocks: The Share of Ownership

Stocks, often referred to as equities or shares, represent ownership in a company. When you buy a stock, you buy a piece of that company. Stocks are traded on stock exchanges, and owning them entitles you to certain rights, such as voting on company decisions and receiving a portion of the company's profits in the form of dividends.

Key Points about Stocks:

1. **Ownership:** Owning a stock means you have a share of ownership in the company, no matter how small.

2. **Value Fluctuations:** Stock prices can fluctuate daily due to various factors, including company performance, market sentiment, and economic conditions.

3. **Risk and Reward:** Stocks offer the potential for high returns but come with higher risk than other investments. The stock market can be volatile.

4. **Dividends:** Some companies pay dividends to shareholders, providing a regular income stream.

5. **Capital Gains:** Investors can profit by selling stocks at a higher price than what they paid, known as capital gains.

Bonds: The Debt Instruments

While stocks represent ownership, bonds are essentially loans that you provide to governments, municipalities, or corporations. When you buy a bond, you are lending your money to the issuer in exchange for periodic interest payments (coupons) and the return of your principal investment at the bond's maturity date.

Key Points about Bonds:

1. **Debt Securities:** Bonds are debt securities, meaning you are a creditor to the issuer, not an owner.

2. **Interest Payments:** Bonds pay periodic interest, typically semiannually, and return the principal at maturity.

3. **Risk and Return:** Bonds are generally considered lower-risk investments compared to stocks, but they offer lower potential returns.

4. **Credit Ratings:** Bonds are assigned credit ratings based on the issuer's creditworthiness. Higher-rated bonds are less risky but offer lower yields.

5. **Diversification:** Bonds can be used to diversify an investment portfolio and manage risk.

Mutual Funds: The Basket of Investments

Mutual funds are investment vehicles that pool money from multiple investors to purchase a diversified portfolio of stocks, bonds, or other securities. They offer investors instant diversification, professional management, and liquidity. Mutual funds are managed by fund managers who make investment decisions on behalf of investors.

Key Points about Mutual Funds:

1. **Diversification:** Mutual funds provide diversification by holding a mix of assets, reducing risk.

2. **Professional Management:** Fund managers make investment decisions based on the fund's objectives.

3. **Liquidity:** Mutual fund shares can typically be bought or sold on any business day at the fund's net asset value (NAV).

4. **Types:** There are various types of mutual funds, including equity funds (investing in stocks), bond funds (investing in bonds), and balanced funds (a mix of stocks and bonds).

5. **Fees:** Mutual funds charge fees, including management fees (expense ratios) and, in some cases, front-end or back-end sales charges (loads).

The Risk-Return Trade-Off: Balancing Act

Investing involves navigating the delicate balance between risk and return. Generally, assets with higher potential returns come with higher risk. Here's how this trade-off plays out:

- **Stocks:** High potential returns, high risk. The stock market can be volatile, with prices subject to rapid fluctuations.

- **Bonds:** Moderate returns, moderate risk. Bonds are generally considered safer than stocks but offer lower potential returns.

- **Mutual Funds:** Risk and return depend on the fund's composition. Equity funds tend to have higher potential returns and higher risk, while bond funds offer lower returns and lower risk.

The Importance of Diversification

Diversification is the strategy of spreading your investments across different asset classes and types to reduce risk. By diversifying, you aim to minimize the impact of poor performance in one investment on your overall portfolio.

Imagine you have a portfolio consisting solely of tech stocks, and the tech sector experiences a downturn. In this scenario, your entire portfolio would suffer. However, if you had a diversified portfolio that included not only tech stocks but also bonds, real estate, and other asset classes, the impact of the tech sector downturn would be less severe.

Building Your Investment Portfolio

Creating an investment portfolio is akin to assembling a puzzle. It involves selecting the right mix of assets to align with your financial goals, risk tolerance, and investment horizon.

Here's a step-by-step guide to building your investment portfolio:

1. Define Your Goals: Start by clarifying your financial objectives. Are you saving for retirement, a home, or education? Knowing your goals will help determine your investment horizon.

2. Assess Your Risk Tolerance: Evaluate your willingness and ability to take on risk. Factors such as age, income, and temperament play a role in determining your risk tolerance.

3. Diversify Your Portfolio: Spread your investments across different asset classes, such as stocks, bonds, real estate, and cash equivalents. Within each asset class, consider diversifying further. For example, in stocks, diversify across industries and geographies.

4. Choose Investments: Select individual stocks, bonds, mutual funds, or exchange-traded funds (ETFs) that align with your goals and risk tolerance.

5. Monitor and Rebalance: Regularly review your portfolio's performance and rebalance if necessary to maintain your target asset allocation.

6. Stay Informed: Keep abreast of market news and developments to make informed decisions.

The Journey Begins: Start Investing Today

As you embark on your investment journey, remember that investing is a long-term endeavor. It requires patience, discipline, and a commitment to your financial goals. Markets may fluctuate, but a well-thought-out investment strategy can weather the storms and lead you to financial growth and success.

Once perceived as a mysterious landscape, the world of investing becomes more accessible when you break it down into its core components—stocks, bonds, and mutual funds. With knowledge and prudent decision-making, you can chart a course to financial prosperity, making your money work for you and turning your financial aspirations into reality.

Risk Tolerance, Diversification, and the Long-Term Perspective

Investing is not merely a financial endeavor; it's a journey filled with decisions that can shape your financial future. To embark on this journey successfully, it's crucial to understand and embrace three key principles: risk tolerance, diversification, and the importance of a long-term perspective. These principles are the compass, the map, and the steady hand on the helm that will guide you through the often turbulent waters of the investment world.

Risk Tolerance: Your Financial Comfort Zone

Risk tolerance is a deeply personal aspect of investing. It reflects your emotional and psychological comfort with the ups and downs of the financial markets. Understanding your risk tolerance is fundamental because it directly influences the composition of your investment portfolio.

1. Factors Influencing Risk Tolerance:

    - **Financial Goals:** Your specific financial objectives play a role. If you have short-term goals like buying a house in a year, your risk tolerance may be lower than someone saving for retirement in 20 years.

    - **Time Horizon:** The length of time you plan to hold your investments matters. Longer horizons generally allow for a higher risk tolerance because there's more time to ride out market fluctuations.

- **Financial Situation:** Your financial circumstances, including income, expenses, and existing investments, influence your risk tolerance. A strong financial position may lead to a higher tolerance for risk.

- **Personality:** Your natural disposition and how you react to financial stress are key factors. Some individuals are naturally risk-averse, while others are more comfortable with risk.

2. Risk Tolerance Categories:

- **Conservative:** Individuals with a low risk tolerance prioritize preserving their capital and are willing to accept lower returns in exchange for reduced risk. They typically invest more in stable assets like bonds and cash equivalents.

- **Moderate:** Moderate risk tolerance individuals seek a balance between risk and return. They are willing to accept some fluctuations in their investments for the potential of higher returns. A typical portfolio may include a mix of stocks and bonds.

- **Aggressive:** Those with a high risk tolerance are willing to take on more risk in pursuit of potentially higher returns. They often have a higher allocation to stocks and may invest in riskier assets.

Understanding your risk tolerance is the first step in building an investment portfolio that aligns with your financial goals and emotional comfort. It ensures you won't lose sleep over market volatility.

Diversification: The Shield Against Volatility

Imagine a ship with multiple sails, each catching the wind from a different direction. Diversification is the equivalent of having those sails—when one falters, the others keep the ship moving. It's a strategy aimed at reducing risk by spreading your investments across a variety of asset classes and securities.

1. Benefits of Diversification:

- **Risk Mitigation:** Diversifying across different assets means your portfolio is less dependent on the performance of any single investment. When some investments falter, others may perform well, offsetting losses.

- **Smoothing Returns:** Diversification can help smooth out the volatility in your portfolio's returns. While some assets may experience sharp declines, others may remain stable or increase in value.

- **Enhanced Consistency:** Diversification fosters consistency in your portfolio's performance, making tracking progress toward your financial goals easier.

2. Diversification Strategies:

- **Asset Classes:** Diversify across major asset classes like stocks, bonds, real estate, and cash equivalents. Each asset class has its risk-return profile.

- **Geographical Diversification:** Invest in assets from different regions and countries to reduce geographic risk. Global diversification can help mitigate the impact of regional economic downturns.

- **Sector Diversification:** Within stocks, consider diversifying across different industry sectors, such as technology, healthcare, and finance.

- **Investment Types:** Diversify within asset classes by investing in a mix of individual stocks, bonds, mutual funds, and exchange-traded funds (ETFs).

While diversification doesn't eliminate risk entirely, it is a powerful tool to manage and mitigate risk in your investment portfolio.

The Long-Term Perspective: Your North Star

Investing is not a sprint; it's a marathon. The long-term perspective is a mindset that acknowledges that markets will fluctuate and temporary setbacks are part of the journey. It's about looking beyond short-term noise and focusing on your ultimate financial goals.

1. **The Power of Time:** Time is an investor's greatest ally. Thanks to the magic of compounding, the longer your investment horizon, the more time your money has to grow. Compound interest can turn modest investments into substantial wealth over time.

2. **Riding Out Volatility:** Short-term market fluctuations are inevitable. However, a long-term perspective allows you to weather market volatility confidently, knowing that markets tend to rise over time.

3. **Avoiding Emotional Decisions:** Emotional reactions to market events can lead to impulsive decisions that harm your portfolio. A long-term perspective helps you stay focused on your goals rather than reacting to short-term market noise.

4. **Staying Committed:** Consistency is key in long-term investing. Regular contributions and adherence to your investment strategy, even during challenging times, are vital to your success.

Remember the famous Warren Buffett adage: "The stock market is a device for transferring money from the impatient to the patient." Embracing a long-term perspective means being among the patient.

Conclusion: A Balanced Approach to Investing

Navigating the world of investing requires a balanced approach that combines an understanding of risk tolerance, diversification, and the importance of a long-term perspective. It's about finding the right balance between risk and reward, protecting your investments against unnecessary volatility, and staying committed to your financial goals.

Ultimately, investing is not a one-size-fits-all endeavor. Your investment strategy should be tailored to your unique financial situation and aspirations. By embracing these principles and crafting an investment plan that aligns with them, you can chart a course toward financial security, growth, and the realization of your dreams. The investment journey may have its challenges, but with the right knowledge and perspective, it can also be a rewarding and fulfilling path to financial success.

Chapter 5: Generating Passive Income Streams

Imagine a life where your money works for you, consistently adding to your wealth without requiring you to trade your time for every dollar earned. This is the magic of passive income—money that comes in regularly with little or no effort on your part. In this article, we'll explore the concept of generating passive income streams, breaking down the basics in simple terms so that you can embark on your journey to financial freedom.

Understanding Passive Income: The Foundation

Passive income is money earned without active involvement. Unlike a traditional job where you exchange your time and effort for a paycheck, passive income comes from assets and investments that generate returns on their own. It's the financial equivalent of setting up a money tree that keeps bearing fruit.

Why Pursue Passive Income?

The allure of passive income lies in its potential to provide financial security, independence, and the freedom to pursue your dreams. Here are some compelling reasons to seek passive income:

1. **Financial Freedom:** Passive income can cover your living expenses, allowing you to work by choice, not necessity.

2. **Diversification:** It diversifies your income sources, reducing reliance on a single job or business.

3. **Wealth Building:** Over time, passive income streams can accumulate, building wealth and assets that can be passed down to future generations.

4. **Flexibility:** Passive income provides flexibility in how and where you work, potentially allowing for more leisure and family time.

Now, let's explore various passive income sources and strategies:

1. Dividend Stocks:

Dividend stocks are shares of companies that pay out a portion of their earnings to shareholders in the form of dividends. By investing in dividend-paying stocks, you can receive regular income while potentially benefiting from capital appreciation.

2. Rental Real Estate:

Owning rental properties is a classic way to earn passive income. Rental income from tenants can provide a steady stream of cash flow, and property values may appreciate over time.

3. Peer-to-Peer Lending:

Platforms like LendingClub and Prosper enable you to lend money to individuals or small businesses in exchange for interest payments. Your investments can be spread across multiple borrowers to reduce risk.

4. Real Estate Investment Trusts (REITs):

REITs are companies that own, operate or finance income-producing real estate properties. Investing in REITs can expose the real estate market without the need for direct property ownership.

5. Bonds:

Bonds pay periodic interest (coupons) to bondholders. By investing in bonds, you can receive regular interest payments until the bond matures, at this point, you get your principal back.

6. Peer-to-Peer Rental Platforms:

Websites like Airbnb and Vrbo allow you to rent out spare rooms or properties for short-term stays. This can be a flexible way to generate income from your existing assets.

7. Create and Sell Digital Products:

If you have expertise in a particular field, you can create and sell digital products like e-books, online courses, or downloadable software. Once created, these products can generate income indefinitely.

8. Stock Photography:

If you enjoy photography, you can sell your photos on stock photography websites. Each time someone purchases one of your photos, you earn a royalty payment.

9. Affiliate Marketing:

Affiliate marketing involves promoting products or services and earning a commission for each sale made through your referral. This can be done through blogs, websites, or social media.

10. Create a YouTube Channel or Blog:

Creating content on platforms like YouTube or a blog can lead to passive income through advertising revenue, sponsored content, and affiliate marketing.

11. Royalties from Intellectual Property:

If you have written a book, composed music, or created art, you can earn royalties when your work is sold or used.

12. Automated Online Businesses:

Some online businesses, like dropshipping or print-on-demand services, can be set up to run on autopilot, requiring minimal ongoing effort.

Building Passive Income Streams: Key Strategies

> **Start Early:** The power of compounding works in your favor when you start early. Even small contributions can grow significantly over time.

Diversify: Don't put all your eggs in one basket. Diversify your passive income sources to reduce risk.

Continuously Learn: Stay updated on investment opportunities, industry trends, and emerging passive income strategies.

Monitor and Adjust: Regularly review your passive income streams to ensure they perform as expected. Make adjustments as needed.

Be Patient: Building substantial passive income takes time and persistence. Avoid get-rich-quick schemes and focus on long-term strategies.

Seek Professional Advice: Depending on your financial situation, it may be wise to consult with a financial advisor or tax professional to optimize your passive income strategy.

The Path to Financial Freedom: Your Journey Begins

Generating passive income is like planting seeds that grow into financial security and freedom. It's about creating multiple streams of income that flow into your life, giving you the flexibility and choices you desire. Whether you dream of early retirement, funding your child's education, or simply enjoying a more comfortable life, passive income can be your ticket to realizing those dreams.

As you embark on your passive income journey, remember that it's not a one-size-fits-all endeavor. Choose strategies that align with your interests, financial goals, and risk tolerance. With patience, dedication, and a commitment to building your passive income streams, you can take significant steps toward achieving financial freedom and living life on your terms. Your financial future is yours to shape, and the journey begins today.

Ways to generate Passive Income

Passive income generation methods offer various ways to earn money with minimal effort or active involvement. Here are three popular passive income sources: real estate, dividends, and online businesses.

1. Real Estate:

Real estate is a tried-and-true method for generating passive income. It involves purchasing properties (such as residential homes, commercial buildings, or rental apartments) and earning income from them. Here's how it works:

> **Rental Properties:** Owning rental properties is a common way to earn passive income. You purchase a property, find tenants, and collect monthly rent payments. You keep the rental income as profit after covering expenses like maintenance, property taxes, and mortgage payments.

> **Real Estate Investment Trusts (REITs):** REITs are an option if you want to invest in real estate without owning physical properties. REITs are companies that own, operate, or finance income-producing real estate. By investing in REITs, you can receive dividends generated from the rental income and capital gains from property sales.

> **Real Estate Crowdfunding:** Real estate crowdfunding platforms allow you to invest in specific real estate projects with other investors. You can invest in residential or commercial properties, typically with a lower initial investment than buying a property outright.

2. Dividends:

Investing in dividend-paying stocks is another way to generate passive income. Many established companies distribute a portion of their earnings to shareholders through dividends. Here's how it works:

Stock Ownership: When you own shares of a dividend-paying company, you become a shareholder. Companies typically pay dividends quarterly or annually, providing you with a steady income stream.

Reinvestment: Many investors choose to reinvest their dividends back into the same stocks, allowing them to benefit from compound growth. This can accelerate the growth of your investment portfolio over time.

Diversification: To reduce risk, diversify your dividend stock holdings across different industries and sectors. This way, your passive income isn't dependent on the performance of a single company.

3. Online Businesses:

The digital age has opened up numerous opportunities for building online businesses that can generate passive income. Here are a few options:

Blogging: Creating a blog around a niche topic you're passionate about can be profitable. You can earn income through advertising, sponsored posts, affiliate marketing, and selling digital products like e-books or online courses.

YouTube Channel: Starting a YouTube channel and creating engaging video content can lead to ad revenue from platforms like Google AdSense. You can also earn money through sponsorships and merchandise sales.

Affiliate Marketing: Promoting products or services through affiliate marketing programs can be lucrative for earning passive income. You earn a commission for each sale made through your referral.

Dropshipping: Running an e-commerce store using a dropshipping model allows you to sell products without the need for inventory. When customers make purchases, the products are shipped directly from the supplier.

Print-on-Demand: Create custom designs for products like T-shirts, mugs, or phone cases and sell them through print-on-demand platforms. You earn a commission on each sale without managing inventory.

Mobile Apps: Developing a mobile app and monetizing it through in-app advertising, subscriptions, or one-time purchases can lead to passive income if the app gains popularity.

These online businesses may require significant upfront work, but once established, they can continue to generate income with minimal ongoing effort.

Choosing the Right Passive Income Source:

The choice of passive income source depends on your financial goals, risk tolerance, and available resources. Here are some considerations:

Diversification: Consider diversifying your passive income sources to spread risk. For example, you might invest in a mix of real estate, dividend stocks, and an online business.

Interest and Expertise: Choose income sources that align with your interests and expertise. Building a successful online business may require a different skill set than managing rental properties.

Time Horizon: Consider your investment horizon. Some passive income sources, like real estate, may require a longer-term commitment.

Initial Capital: Evaluate your available capital. Some sources, like dividend stocks, may require less upfront investment than purchasing real estate.

Risk Tolerance: Assess your risk tolerance. Investments in stocks and online businesses can be more volatile than real estate.

Remember that passive income doesn't mean completely hands-off. You may still need to oversee investments, manage tenants, or occasionally update your online business. However, compared to active income sources like a full-time job, passive income offers greater flexibility and the potential for financial independence. Explore your options and build a diversified portfolio of passive income streams that align with your financial goals.

Creating passive income sources requires careful planning and execution. Here are actionable steps to get started:

1. Define Your Financial Goals:

> Determine your financial objectives and the level of passive income you aim to generate. Are you looking for supplementary income, early retirement, or long-term wealth building? Be specific about your goals.

2. Assess Your Current Financial Situation:

> Take a close look at your current financial position, including income, expenses, debts, and existing investments. Understand how much you can allocate toward creating passive income sources.

3. Identify Your Passive Income Sources:

> Based on your goals and financial situation, explore different passive income options such as real estate, dividend stocks, bonds, online businesses, or intellectual property.

4. Conduct Research:

> Dive deep into the passive income source you're interested in. Understand the risks, potential returns, and requirements. Research specific investments, markets, or industries related to your chosen source.

5. Create a Passive Income Strategy:

Develop a well-thought-out plan that outlines your passive income strategy. Determine how much you need to invest, your expected returns, and your investment horizon.

6. Set a Budget:

Establish a budget that allocates funds for creating passive income sources. Consider how much you can invest initially and how much you can contribute regularly.

7. Reduce Debt and Save:

Before investing, prioritize paying off high-interest debts. Reducing debt can free up more funds for investments. Additionally, build an emergency fund to cover unexpected expenses.

8. Build a Diversified Portfolio:

Diversification is key to managing risk. Spread your investments across different passive income sources and asset classes to reduce vulnerability to market fluctuations.

9. Explore Passive Income Streams:

Based on your chosen sources, start taking actionable steps:

For Real Estate: Research properties, assess potential rental income, and consider financing options. Seek advice from real estate professionals if necessary.

For Dividend Stocks: Open a brokerage account, research dividend-paying companies, and start investing in dividend stocks.

For Bonds: Set up an account with a brokerage or use a bond mutual fund or ETF to invest in bonds.

For Online Businesses: Identify your niche, create a business plan, and set up your online presence. This may include creating a website, starting a blog, or launching an e-commerce store.

For Intellectual Property: Consider patenting or copyrighting your work, or explore platforms that allow you to license or sell your intellectual property.

10. Automate Investments:

Set up automatic contributions to your chosen investments. Consistency is key to building passive income over time.

11. Monitor and Adjust:

Regularly review the performance of your passive income sources. Ensure that your investments are aligning with your goals and making necessary adjustments.

12. Reinvest and Compound:

Whenever possible, reinvest your passive income earnings. This allows your investments to grow exponentially through the power of compounding.

13. Seek Professional Advice:

Depending on the complexity of your passive income strategy and investments, consider consulting with financial advisors, real estate experts, or legal professionals to ensure you're making informed decisions.

14. Be Patient and Persistent:

Generating significant passive income often takes time. Be patient, stay committed to your strategy, and resist the urge to make impulsive decisions based on short-term market fluctuations.

15. Track Your Progress:

> Regularly track your passive income earnings and monitor your progress toward your financial goals. Adjust your strategy as needed to stay on course.

Creating passive income sources requires diligence, patience, and a strategic approach. By following these actionable steps and continuously educating yourself about your chosen income streams, you can work towards achieving financial independence and enjoying the benefits of passive income.

Chapter 6: Navigating Debt and Credit

Debt and credit are two interconnected aspects of personal finance that significantly influence financial well-being. When managed wisely, they can be valuable tools that help you achieve your financial goals. However, mishandling them can lead to financial stress and setbacks. In this article, we'll explore the world of debt and credit, providing you with a roadmap to navigate these financial aspects effectively.

Understanding Debt: The Double-Edged Sword

Debt is borrowed money you promise to repay, typically with interest, over time. It comes in various forms, including credit cards, loans, mortgages, and lines of credit. Depending on its use, debt can be both a valuable financial tool and a potential trap.

Good Debt vs. Bad Debt:

> **Good Debt:** This type of debt is used to invest in assets that have the potential to grow in value or generate income over time. Examples include:
>
>> **Mortgages:** Buying a home can be considered good debt because real estate tends to appreciate in value.
>>
>> **Student Loans:** Education loans are an investment in your future earning potential.
>>
>> **Business Loans:** Borrowing to start or expand a business can be wise if it leads to increased income.
>
> **Bad Debt:** This type of debt is typically used to finance purchases that depreciate quickly and do not generate income. Examples include:

Credit Card Debt: High-interest credit card debt used for non-essential purchases can quickly become a financial burden.

Consumer Loans: Financing vacations, luxury items, or electronics with high-interest loans falls into the bad debt category.

Navigating Debt Effectively:

Prioritize High-Interest Debt: If you have high-interest debt, such as credit card balances, prioritize paying it off as quickly as possible. High-interest rates can accumulate rapidly and hinder your financial progress.

Create a Repayment Plan: Develop a debt repayment plan that outlines how much you'll pay each month and when you'll be debt-free. Stick to this plan consistently.

Budget Wisely: Create a realistic budget for debt repayment and essential expenses. Cutting non-essential spending can free up more money for debt reduction.

Emergency Fund: Build an emergency fund to cover unexpected expenses, so you don't rely on credit when financial surprises occur.

Understanding Credit: Your Financial Reputation

Credit is your financial reputation. It's a measure of your ability to borrow money and repay it. Lenders use your credit history and credit score to assess your creditworthiness when you apply for loans or credit cards. Here's how credit works:

Credit Report: Your credit history is recorded in a credit report, which includes information about your credit accounts, payment history, and any negative marks like late payments or defaults.

Credit Score: Your credit score is a numerical representation of your creditworthiness. It's calculated based on your credit history. A higher score indicates better creditworthiness.

Credit Types: There are different types of credit, including revolving credit (credit cards), installment credit (loans with fixed payments), and open credit (like lines of credit).

Building and Maintaining Good Credit:

Pay Bills on Time: Consistently paying your bills and debts on time is critical to building good credit.

Use Credit Wisely: Avoid maxing out credit cards and using credit for unnecessary purchases. A general guideline is to keep credit card balances below 30% of your credit limit.

Monitor Your Credit: Regularly check your credit report for errors or discrepancies. You can obtain free credit reports from the major credit bureaus each year.

Diverse Credit Mix: Having a mix of credit types (e.g., credit cards, loans) can positively impact your credit score.

Long Credit History: The length of your credit history matters. Keep older accounts open, even if you don't use them often.

Balancing Debt and Credit: Your Financial Harmony

To navigate debt and credit effectively, it's essential to balance responsible borrowing and maintaining a favourable credit profile. Here are some tips to achieve this balance:

Use Debt Strategically: Borrow for investments that have the potential to increase your net worth, like education or real estate. Avoid accumulating bad debt for non-essential purchases.

Manage Credit Utilization: Keep your credit card balances low in relation to your credit limits. High credit utilization can negatively affect your credit score.

Stay Informed: Educate yourself about the terms and conditions of your loans and credit cards. Understand interest rates, fees, and due dates.

Set Financial Goals: Establish clear financial goals and create a plan for achieving them. Use credit and debt as tools to reach these goals, not as crutches.

Seek Professional Advice: If you're struggling with debt, consider speaking with a financial advisor or credit counselor who can provide guidance and solutions.

Debt and credit are integral parts of modern financial life. When managed wisely, they can help you achieve your financial goals, whether buying a home, starting a business, or pursuing an education. By understanding the differences between good and bad debt, effectively managing debt, and maintaining good credit, you can build a solid financial foundation and confidently navigate your financial journey. Remember that financial harmony is achieved through knowledge, discipline, and a clear plan for your financial future.

Managing Debt

Managing and reducing debt effectively is a crucial step toward achieving financial well-being and ultimately, financial freedom. Here's a comprehensive guide to help you take control of your debt:

1. Assess Your Debt:

Start by gathering all your financial statements, including credit card bills, loan statements, and any other debt-related documents. List each debt's outstanding balance, interest rate, and minimum monthly payment.

2. Create a Budget:

> Develop a detailed budget that outlines your monthly income and expenses. Identify areas where you can cut discretionary spending to allocate more funds toward debt repayment.

3. Prioritize High-Interest Debt:

> Focus on paying off high-interest debts first. These are often credit card debts or payday loans with interest rates that can accumulate quickly.

4. Set Clear Debt Repayment Goals:

> Establish specific, measurable, and achievable goals for paying off your debts. For example, set a goal to pay off a certain credit card balance in six months.

5. Snowball vs. Avalanche Method:

> Choose a debt repayment strategy that suits your psychology and financial situation.

> **Snowball Method:** Pay off your smallest debt first while making minimum payments on others. Once it's paid off, roll the amount you were paying into the next smallest debt. This method provides psychological wins as you eliminate debts one by one.

> **Avalanche Method:** First, pay off debts with the highest interest rates. This method minimizes the overall interest you pay.

6. Negotiate Lower Interest Rates:

> Contact your creditors to inquire about the possibility of lowering your interest rates. A good payment history and a polite request can sometimes lead to lower rates.

7. Consolidate and Refinance:

If you have multiple high-interest debts, consider consolidating them into a single, lower-interest loan. This can make your debt more manageable and potentially save on interest.

8. Create an Emergency Fund:

While repaying debt is essential, having an emergency fund can prevent you from relying on credit in case of unexpected expenses. Start by saving a small amount each month until you have at least $1,000 in your emergency fund.

9. Increase Your Income:

Explore opportunities to increase your income, such as working part-time, freelancing, or selling unused items. Use this extra income to accelerate debt repayment.

10. Avoid New Debt:

While repaying existing debts, avoid taking on new debt. This includes resisting the temptation to use credit cards for unnecessary purchases.

11. Seek Professional Help:

If you're overwhelmed by your debt or struggling to make payments, consider contacting a credit counselling agency. They can help you create a debt management plan and negotiate with creditors on your behalf.

12. Stay Committed:

Debt repayment requires discipline and patience. Stay committed to your plan even when progress seems slow. Celebrate small victories along the way to stay motivated.

13. Track Your Progress:

> Regularly monitor your debt reduction progress. As you see your balances decrease, you'll gain confidence and motivation to keep going.

14. Avoid Bankruptcy as a Last Resort:

> Bankruptcy should only be considered as a last resort when all other options have been exhausted. It has significant long-term consequences on your credit and financial future.

15. Educate Yourself:

> Continuously educate yourself about personal finance, budgeting, and debt management. Understanding the financial principles and strategies can empower you to make informed decisions.

Remember that managing and reducing debt is a journey that requires time and persistence. Stay committed to your goals, and don't be discouraged by setbacks. As you steadily reduce your debt, you'll gain control of your finances and set the stage for a more secure financial future.

Mastering Credit

Credit cards can be powerful financial tools when used responsibly. They provide convenience, financial flexibility, and the opportunity to build and maintain a strong credit score. This comprehensive guide will explore responsible credit card usage, the ins and outs of credit scores, and strategies to improve and maintain your creditworthiness.

Understanding Your Credit Score:

A credit score is a numerical representation of your creditworthiness. Lenders use a three-digit number to assess the risk of lending to you. The most widely used credit scoring models are FICO® and VantageScore®. Your credit score is based on several factors:

Payment History (35%): This is the most significant factor in your credit score. It reflects whether you've made on-time payments, missed payments, or defaulted on loans.

Credit Utilization (30%): This measures the percentage of your available credit that you're using. A lower utilization rate is better for your score.

Length of Credit History (15%): Longer credit histories generally result in higher scores.

Types of Credit (10%): A mix of different types of credit, such as credit cards, loans, and mortgages, can positively impact your score.

New Credit Inquiries (10%): Opening multiple new credit accounts quickly can hurt your score.

Maintaining a Strong Credit Score:

Pay Bills On Time: Consistently pay your bills and credit card balances on or before the due date. Late payments can significantly damage your credit score.

Monitor Credit Utilization: Keep your credit card balances below your credit limits. A utilisation rate below 30% is generally recommended.

Avoid Opening Unnecessary Accounts: While a mix of credit types can be beneficial, avoid opening too many new accounts within a short period, as this can lower your score.

Keep Old Accounts Open: The length of your credit history matters. Keep older credit card accounts open, even if you don't use them often.

Regularly Check Your Credit Report: Review your credit reports from the three major credit bureaus (Equifax, Experian, and TransUnion) at least once a year to check for errors or discrepancies.

Use Credit Responsibly: Only use credit cards for monthly purchases you can afford to pay off in full. Avoid carrying high balances or revolving debt.

Diversify Credit Types: Consider different types of credit, such as installment loans (e.g., auto loans) and revolving credit (e.g., credit cards), to demonstrate responsible credit usage.

Strategies to Increase Your Credit Score:

Reduce Outstanding Debt: Pay down high-interest debts and focus on reducing credit card balances.

Negotiate with Creditors: If you have past-due accounts or collections, consider negotiating with creditors or collection agencies to settle debts or set up payment plans.

Become an Authorized User: Ask a family member or friend with a good credit history to add you as an authorized user on their credit card account. This can help boost your credit score.

Apply for New Credit Sparingly: Opening too many new credit accounts quickly can hurt your score. Apply for new credit only when necessary.

Check for Errors: Regularly review your credit reports for inaccuracies and dispute any errors with the credit bureaus.

Factors That Can Impact Your Credit Negatively:

Late Payments: Missed or late payments on loans, credit cards, or bills can have a significant negative impact on your credit score.

High Credit Card Balances: Carrying high credit card balances relative to your credit limits can lower your score.

Defaulting on Loans: Defaulting on loans or declaring bankruptcy can severely damage your credit score.

Collections: Having accounts sent to collections due to non-payment can result in negative marks on your credit report.

Frequent Credit Applications: Applying for credit too often can be viewed as risky behavior and lower your score.

Closing Old Accounts: Closing old credit card accounts can shorten your credit history, potentially impacting your score.

Responsible credit card usage and understanding your credit score are essential for financial well-being. A strong credit score can open doors to better loan terms, lower interest rates, and increased financial opportunities. By consistently practicing good financial habits, paying bills on time, and monitoring your credit, you can build and maintain a strong credit profile that serves as a valuable financial asset. Remember that improving your credit score takes time, patience, and discipline, but the long-term benefits are worth the effort.

Chapter 7: Protecting Your Financial Future: Insurance and Emergency Funds

Your financial future is a tapestry of dreams, goals, and security. To safeguard this future, you must weave a strong foundation of financial resilience. Life is rife with uncertainties, from unexpected emergencies to economic fluctuations. It's crucial to prepare for these challenges and fortify your financial well-being.

Build an Emergency Fund: Start by creating a robust emergency fund. This financial cushion provides a safety net during unexpected crises, such as medical bills, car repairs, or job loss. Aim to save at least three to six months' worth of living expenses.

Invest in Insurance: Insurance is a critical shield for your financial future. Health, life, auto, and homeowners or renters insurance can protect you from overwhelming financial burdens in times of crisis. Carefully review and update your coverage as needed.

Establish a Budget: A well-structured budget is your financial roadmap. It helps you control spending, save, and invest wisely. Regularly review and adjust your budget to align with your financial goals and changing circumstances.

Diversify Your Investments: Investment diversification spreads risk and helps protect your financial future. Allocate your investments across different asset classes, such as stocks, bonds, and real estate, to reduce vulnerability to market fluctuations.

Plan for Retirement: Your financial future extends beyond the present. Saving for retirement is a long-term endeavor. Contribute to retirement accounts like a 401(k) or IRA, taking advantage of employer matches and tax benefits.

Minimize Debt: Manage and reduce debt effectively. High-interest debts can erode your financial future. Prioritize paying off debts, starting with those carrying the highest interest rates.

Educate Yourself: Financial literacy is your armor against unexpected challenges. Continuously educate yourself about personal finance, investments, and retirement planning. Seek professional advice when necessary.

Estate Planning: Protect your legacy by creating a comprehensive estate plan. This includes drafting a will, establishing trusts, and designating beneficiaries for your assets and accounts.

Stay Healthy: Health is a cornerstone of financial security. Invest in a healthy lifestyle, maintain adequate health insurance, and plan for healthcare costs in retirement.

Adapt to Change: Life is dynamic. Your financial future depends on your ability to adapt to change. Be prepared to adjust your financial strategies in response to new circumstances.

Avoid Impulse Spending: Temptations are plentiful in today's consumer-driven world. Practice restraint and avoid impulse spending that can undermine your financial future.

Continuously Assess and Reevaluate: Regularly review your financial goals and strategies. Life's twists and turns may require adjustments to your plans.

Seek Professional Guidance: Financial advisors can provide invaluable guidance in protecting your financial future. Consider consulting with professionals to navigate complex financial decisions.

Foster Healthy Financial Habits: Instill healthy financial habits in your daily life. Save consistently, invest wisely, and live within your means. These habits are the building blocks of financial resilience.

Stay Positive and Resilient: Maintain a positive outlook on your financial future. Resilience in the face of challenges is a powerful tool for ensuring lasting financial security.

Monitor Your Credit: Regularly check your credit reports to ensure accuracy and detect signs of identity theft or unauthorized activity. A strong credit history is a valuable asset for your financial future.

Prepare for Major Life Events: Life events like marriage, the birth of a child, or sending a child to college can impact your finances. Plan for these milestones, adjusting your budget and savings accordingly.

Save for Large Expenses: Set aside funds for major expenses such as a home down payment, a new car, or a dream vacation. Avoid relying on credit for these purchases, which can lead to debt accumulation.

Consider Long-Term Care Planning: As you age, long-term care expenses may become a significant part of your financial future. Explore options like long-term care insurance to mitigate this potential burden.

Embrace Tax-Efficient Strategies: Minimize your tax liabilities by exploring tax-efficient investment strategies and taking advantage of tax-advantaged accounts like IRAs and HSAs.

Protect Against Identity Theft: Identity theft can wreak havoc on your finances. Safeguard your personal information, monitor your accounts for suspicious activity, and consider identity theft protection services.

Stay Informed About Financial Markets: Understand the impact of economic events on your investments. Keeping up with financial news can help you make informed decisions about your portfolio.

Encourage Financial Literacy in Your Family: Teach your children and family members about responsible financial habits. Passing on financial knowledge ensures a secure financial future for your loved ones.

Prepare for the Unexpected: While no one likes to think about it, consider estate planning and end-of-life decisions. Establishing a clear plan can relieve your loved ones of added stress during challenging times.

Seek Financial Balance: Balancing your financial priorities is key. Don't focus solely on the future while neglecting present needs, and vice versa. Finding equilibrium ensures a well-rounded financial life.

Remember that protecting your financial future is an ongoing process. Adaptability, vigilance, and prudent financial decisions are your allies in navigating the uncertainties of life. As you implement these strategies and build resilience, you'll be better prepared to face whatever financial challenges or opportunities come your way.

Insurance: Safeguarding Your Financial Security

Insurance is a financial arrangement that is pivotal in securing your financial future and peace of mind. It acts as a safety net, protecting you from the financial repercussions of unexpected events or losses. This article will explore what insurance is and why it is paramount to maintaining your financial security.

Understanding Insurance:

At its core, insurance is a contract between you (the policyholder) and an insurance company. In exchange for regular premium payments, the insurer promises to provide financial protection and support in case of specific events or losses. These events, often called "insurable risks," can encompass a wide range of situations, from car accidents and medical emergencies to natural disasters and property damage.

Types of Insurance:

There is a multitude of insurance types designed to address various aspects of life and property:

Health Insurance: Covers medical expenses, ensuring you have access to quality healthcare without crippling financial burdens.

Auto Insurance: Provides protection in case of accidents, damage, or theft involving your vehicle.

Homeowners or Renters Insurance: Safeguards your home or belongings from damage, theft, or other perils.

Life Insurance: Ensures financial support for your loved ones during your passing.

Disability Insurance: Offers income replacement if you become disabled and cannot work.

Property Insurance: Protects your assets, including real estate, against damages from fire, storms, or other disasters.

Travel Insurance: Covers unforeseen expenses while traveling, such as trip cancellations, medical emergencies, or lost luggage.

The Importance of Insurance for Financial Security:

Risk Mitigation: Life is fraught with uncertainties, and unexpected events can strike anytime. Insurance acts as a safety cushion, mitigating the financial impact of these unforeseen circumstances. Without insurance, you risk depleting your savings or going into debt to cover the costs.

Asset Protection: For most individuals, their home, car, and personal belongings are substantial investments. Insurance safeguards these assets, ensuring you won't suffer devastating losses in accidents, theft, or natural disasters.

Healthcare Access: Health insurance is instrumental in providing access to medical care and treatment without the burden of exorbitant medical bills. It allows you to focus on your recovery rather than worrying about the financial toll of healthcare.

Family Security: Life insurance serves as a financial safety net for your family in the event of your untimely demise. It can cover funeral expenses, and outstanding debts, and provide ongoing support for your loved ones.

Legal Requirements: In many cases, insurance is not just a choice but a legal requirement. For example, auto insurance is mandatory in most states to ensure drivers can cover the costs of accidents they may cause.

Peace of Mind: Knowing that you have insurance in place offers peace of mind. It allows you to confidently navigate life's uncertainties, knowing you have a financial buffer to rely on.

Risk Sharing: Insurance operates on the principle of risk sharing. Many policyholders collectively contribute to a pool from which claims are paid. This spreads the financial burden, making coverage more affordable for individuals.

Insurance is not merely a financial product; it's a shield that guards your financial security and that of your loved ones. It offers protection against life's unpredictable twists and turns, allowing you to weather storms with resilience. While insurance premiums may represent a monthly expense, they are an investment in safeguarding your financial future, ensuring that you can navigate life's uncertainties with confidence and security.

Building and Maintaining Emergency Funds: Your Financial Lifeline

Life has a way of throwing unexpected curveballs your way. Financial emergencies can strike when you least expect them, whether it's a sudden medical expense, car repair, or job loss. That's where having an emergency fund comes to the rescue. In this article, we'll explore the importance of building and maintaining an emergency fund and provide insights into how to do it effectively.

The Essence of an Emergency Fund:

An emergency fund is a designated savings account that serves as a financial safety net for unexpected expenses or emergencies. Its primary purpose is to cover urgent, unanticipated costs that may otherwise jeopardize your financial stability. Having an emergency fund means you won't need to rely on credit cards, loans, or deplete your long-term savings when life takes an unexpected turn.

The Importance of an Emergency Fund:

Financial Security: An emergency fund provides a buffer against financial instability. It ensures you can meet essential expenses, such as housing, groceries, and utilities, even when faced with unexpected costs.

Stress Reduction: Knowing you have a financial cushion can significantly reduce stress during challenging times. You can focus on resolving the situation without the added burden of financial worry.

Avoiding Debt: People often borrow money to cover unexpected expenses without an emergency fund. This can lead to debt accumulation and financial strain in the long run.

Building Your Emergency Fund:

Set Clear Goals: Determine how much you want to save in your emergency fund. A common guideline is to aim for three to six months' worth of living expenses, but your personal circumstances may vary.

Create a Budget: Develop a comprehensive budget that tracks your income and expenses. Identify areas where you can cut discretionary spending to allocate funds toward your emergency fund.

Automate Savings: Set up automatic transfers from your checking account to your emergency fund. Treating savings like a non-negotiable expense ensures consistent contributions.

Start Small: If saving a substantial amount seems daunting, start small. Even saving a modest amount each month can gradually build a meaningful emergency fund over time.

Use Windfalls Wisely: Allocate unexpected windfalls, such as tax refunds or bonuses, directly to your emergency fund to boost its growth.

Maintaining Your Emergency Fund:

Avoid Temptation: Your emergency fund is not a rainy-day fund for discretionary spending. Resist the urge to dip into it for non-urgent expenses.

Regularly Review and Adjust: Periodically reassess your financial situation and adjust your emergency fund savings goals as needed. Changes in income, expenses, or family circumstances may necessitate adjustments.

Replenish After Use: If you need to tap into your emergency fund for a genuine emergency, prioritise replenishing the withdrawn amount as soon as possible.

Keep It Liquid: Keep your emergency fund in a highly liquid and easily accessible account, such as a savings account or money market account. You want to access the funds swiftly when needed.

Review and Reduce Expenses: Continue reviewing your budget for opportunities to reduce expenses, which can free up more money for your emergency fund.

Building and maintaining an emergency fund is essential to achieving financial security and peace of mind. Life's uncertainties are inevitable, but having a financial cushion in an emergency fund allows you to navigate these challenges confidently. Start small, automate your savings, and stay committed to your goals. Your emergency fund is not just a financial asset; it's your lifeline when unexpected expenses arise.

Chapter 8: Advanced Strategies for Financial Growth

In the ever-evolving landscape of personal finance, the journey towards financial growth is marked by milestones and opportunities. As you ascend the ladder of financial success, you encounter the basics of budgeting, saving, and investing and advanced strategies that can catapult your financial well-being to new heights. In this introduction, we embark on a journey to explore these advanced strategies, unveiling the pathways to remarkable financial growth.

Beyond the Basics: The Quest for Financial Mastery

For many, the initial steps in personal finance involve budgeting, eliminating debt, and establishing a solid savings foundation. These fundamental principles lay the groundwork for financial stability, creating a safety net that protects against the unexpected and offers the freedom to envision and pursue future goals.

However, financial growth doesn't end with these fundamentals. It's an ongoing process, and as your financial acumen deepens, you'll encounter advanced strategies that can maximize your wealth-building potential. These strategies go beyond the conventional and often involve calculated risks, diversified investments, and a comprehensive understanding of the financial landscape.

Types of Advanced Strategies: Exploring New Horizons

The realm of advanced financial strategies encompasses a diverse range of approaches, each tailored to specific goals and risk tolerances. Among the advanced strategies we'll explore are:

Investment Diversification: Beyond basic stock and bond investments, advanced investors delve into alternative assets, real estate, and even venture capital. Diversification across different asset classes can help manage risk and enhance returns.

Tax Optimization: Advanced strategies often involve intricate tax planning, including strategies like tax-efficient investing, estate tax minimization, and the use of tax-advantaged accounts to optimize overall returns.

Retirement Planning: Advanced retirement planning involves strategies for maximizing retirement savings, optimizing Social Security benefits, and ensuring a comfortable retirement lifestyle.

Risk Management: More sophisticated risk management techniques may include hedging strategies to protect against market volatility or using insurance products to mitigate various risks.

Entrepreneurship and Business Ventures: Beyond traditional employment, advanced strategies may involve entrepreneurship, investing in startups, or even acquiring businesses as avenues for wealth creation.

Estate and Legacy Planning: Crafting a comprehensive estate plan that includes trusts, charitable giving, and generational wealth transfer strategies is crucial for those seeking to leave a lasting financial legacy.

Passive Income Streams: Advanced investors often explore opportunities to generate passive income through investments in dividend-paying stocks, real estate rentals, or other income-producing assets.

Behavioral Finance: Understanding the psychology of financial decision-making can be an advanced strategy in itself. Behavioral finance explores how emotions and cognitive biases influence investment choices.

As we venture deeper into the world of advanced financial strategies, it's essential to approach these opportunities with knowledge, prudence, and a clear understanding of your financial goals and risk tolerance. These strategies are not one-size-fits-all; they are tools to be wielded strategically in pursuit of your unique financial aspirations. In the upcoming sections of this guide, we will delve into each of these advanced strategies, equipping you with the knowledge and insights needed to navigate the intricate landscape of advanced financial growth and empowerment.

In this exploration, we dive deeper into advanced investment strategies, including tax-efficient investing and retirement planning, two crucial pillars that can significantly impact your financial future.

Tax-Efficient Investing: Navigating the Tax Landscape

Tax efficiency in investing is a nuanced strategy that focuses on optimizing your investment returns while minimizing the impact of taxes. In this advanced approach, the goal is not merely to earn returns on your investments but to retain a larger portion of those returns by strategically managing your tax liabilities.

Strategies for Tax-Efficient Investing:

Tax-Advantaged Accounts: Maximizing the use of tax-advantaged accounts like 401(k)s, IRAs, and Health Savings Accounts (HSAs) can reduce your taxable income and shelter your investments from immediate taxation.

Asset Location: Efficiently allocating assets between taxable and tax-advantaged accounts based on their tax treatment can help minimize annual tax liabilities.

Tax-Loss Harvesting: Capitalizing on investment losses by strategically selling assets can offset gains and reduce taxable income.

Long-Term Capital Gains: Holding investments for the long term often results in lower capital gains tax rates compared to short-term gains.

Municipal Bonds: Investing in municipal bonds can provide tax-free interest income, particularly advantageous for those in higher tax brackets.

Qualified Dividend Stocks: Some dividend stocks qualify for preferential tax rates, making them a tax-efficient income source.

Retirement Planning: Paving the Path to Financial Freedom

Advanced retirement planning extends far beyond setting aside funds in a 401(k) or IRA. It's a comprehensive strategy that encompasses various aspects, from maximizing retirement contributions to crafting a retirement income plan that ensures a comfortable and secure post-working life.

Elements of Advanced Retirement Planning:

Maximizing Retirement Contributions: Contributing the maximum allowable amount to retirement accounts, taking full advantage of employer matches, and exploring catch-up contributions as you near retirement age.

Social Security Optimization: Understanding the complexities of Social Security benefits and strategizing when to start claiming to maximize your monthly income.

Longevity Planning: Creating a retirement income plan that considers the possibility of a long retirement, addressing potential healthcare costs and inflation.

Diversified Income Streams: Building diverse income streams for retirement, which may include investments, rental income, annuities, and part-time work.

Healthcare Planning: Preparing for healthcare expenses in retirement, including exploring Medicare and supplemental insurance options.

Estate and Legacy Planning: Ensuring your assets are managed and distributed according to your wishes, minimizing estate taxes, and creating a financial legacy for heirs.

Conclusion: Guiding Your Financial Journey

These advanced investment strategies, tax-efficient investing, and retirement planning are vital components in the journey towards financial prosperity and security. They require financial acumen and a strategic mindset considering long-term goals, tax implications, and the evolving financial landscape.

As you delve deeper into these advanced strategies, remember that your financial path is unique, and these tools can be customized to suit your individual circumstances and aspirations. With the right knowledge and a well-crafted financial plan, you can confidently navigate the intricate terrain of tax-efficient investing and retirement planning, setting the stage for a fulfilling and secure financial future.

Chapter 9: Putting It All Together: Creating Your Financial Freedom Plan

Picture a life where financial worries are but distant echoes, where your resources meet your daily needs and liberate you to pursue your most cherished aspirations. This is the essence of financial freedom—a state where your financial well-being transcends the mundane and propels you towards the extraordinary.

However, achieving financial freedom is not a matter of chance; it's a journey that demands more than the simple accumulation of wealth. It's about crafting a meticulously designed roadmap that aligns with your unique aspirations and circumstances. In this section, we embark on an exploration that consolidates the multifaceted elements of personal finance, leading you through the artistry of crafting your personalized financial freedom plan.

Financial freedom isn't a mere numerical target; it's a lifestyle, a mindset, and a declaration of autonomy over your financial destiny. It's the assurance that you can navigate life's unpredictable terrain with poise and vigor, that you can pursue your passions without the looming shadow of financial constraints.

This journey commences with an appreciation of the fundamental pillars of personal finance, but it extends far beyond them. It encompasses budgeting for financial control, savings for financial resilience, investments for financial growth, and passive income for financial liberation. It explores advanced strategies, tax-efficient investing, and retirement planning, each contributing to your financial tapestry.

Your financial freedom plan is not just a practical manual; it's a canvas on which you paint the vivid picture of your financial future. This guide isn't about following a rigid formula but providing you with the knowledge and tools to forge your unique path to prosperity.

We'll delve into the intricate interplay of financial principles, offering insights and actionable steps. We'll empower you to make informed decisions as you traverse this multifaceted landscape. We'll unlock the world of investments, demystifying terminology and illuminating pathways to wealth. We'll discuss risk tolerance, diversification, and the vital role of a long-term perspective in sculpting your financial masterpiece.

Yet, this guide is more than an archive of financial wisdom; it's a transformative odyssey. It's an invitation to seize the reins of your financial destiny, to cast off the chains of financial worry, and to embrace a life where abundance is not just a dream but a tangible reality.

Remember, your financial goals are as distinct as your fingerprint, and your journey towards financial freedom will mirror your dreams, values, and vision for the future. Whether you stand at the starting line, wrestle with debt, or seek to optimize your financial strategies, this guide is your steadfast companion.

Understanding the Components:

Before we embark on crafting your financial freedom plan, let's recap some of the key components we've explored:

Budgeting and Savings: These foundational pillars are essential for managing your day-to-day finances, establishing an emergency fund, and saving for short-term and long-term goals.

Investing: Advanced investment strategies, such as tax-efficient investing and retirement planning, are crucial for growing your wealth over time and securing your financial future.

Debt Management: Strategies for managing and reducing debt effectively are vital to your overall financial well-being.

Insurance: Protecting your financial security with various insurance types ensures you're prepared for unexpected events or losses.

Passive Income: Building multiple passive income streams, from investments to side businesses, can accelerate your journey to financial freedom.

Risk Management: Understanding and mitigating financial risks, from investment volatility to emergencies, is fundamental to long-term financial success.

Creating Your Financial Freedom Plan:

Define Your Goals: Begin by setting clear and specific financial goals. Whether it's early retirement, buying a home, starting a business, or funding your children's education, your goals will guide your financial plan.

Assess Your Current Financial Situation: Take a close look at your current income, expenses, assets, liabilities, and investments. Understand your net worth and cash flow to identify areas for improvement.

Establish a Budget: Create a detailed budget that aligns with your financial goals. Allocate funds for essential expenses, savings, investments, and debt repayment.

Build Emergency and Opportunity Funds: Prioritize building an emergency fund to cover unexpected expenses. Consider creating an opportunity fund for investments or ventures that align with your goals.

Invest Wisely: Implement advanced investment strategies, including tax-efficient investing and retirement planning, to grow your wealth strategically.

Manage Debt: Develop a plan to manage and reduce debt effectively. Prioritize high-interest debts while maintaining a healthy credit score.

Diversify Income Streams: Explore opportunities for generating passive income, which can provide financial stability and accelerate your path to financial freedom.

Risk Assessment and Mitigation: Identify potential financial risks and develop strategies to mitigate them. This may include insurance, diversifying investments, and emergency preparedness.

Regularly Review and Adjust: Your financial freedom plan is not static. Regularly review your progress, adjust your strategies as needed, and stay committed to your goals.

Seek Professional Guidance: When necessary, consult with financial advisors, tax professionals, and estate planners to ensure your plan aligns with your long-term objectives.

Conclusion: Your Financial Freedom Awaits

Your journey to financial freedom is a path of continuous growth and empowerment. Crafting a comprehensive financial freedom plan, informed by our explored components, empowers you to take control of your financial future. It's not just about reaching a destination but also about enjoying the journey and having the resources to live life on your terms.

Remember that financial freedom is not a one-size-fits-all concept. Your plan should reflect your unique goals, values, and aspirations. As you navigate this journey, stay committed to the principles of financial discipline, adaptability, and lifelong learning. With your personalized financial freedom plan, you're well-equipped to transform your financial dreams into a tangible and fulfilling reality.

Financial Planning Templates and Worksheets

Budgeting Worksheet

Category	Planned Budget	Actual Expenses
Housing	$	$
Utilities	$	$
Transportation	$	$
Groceries	$	$
Dining Out	$	$
Entertainment	$	$
Savings/Investing	$	$
Debt Payments	$	$
Miscellaneous	$	$
Total	$	$

Emergency Fund Tracker

Month/Year	Target Amount	Current Balance	Amount to Save
Month 1	$	$	$
Month 2	$	$	$
Month 3	$	$	$
Month 4	$	$	$
Month 5	$	$	$
Month 6	$	$	$

Investment Goal Tracker

Investment Goal	Target Amount	Current Balance	Amount Left to Reach Goal
Retirement	$	$	$
Home Purchase	$	$	$
Education	$	$	$
Other	$	$	$

Debt Reduction Plan

Debt Account	Starting Balance	Current Balance	Minimum Payment	Extra Payment	Progress
Credit Card 1	$	$	$	$	
Credit Card 2	$	$	$	$	
Student Loan	$	$	$	$	
Car Loan	$	$	$	$	
Personal Loan	$	$	$	$	
Total	$	$	$	$	

These templates and worksheets can serve as valuable tools for readers to assess their financial situation, set goals, track progress, and make informed decisions about their finances. Readers can customize these tables according to their specific needs and financial goals.

Chapter 10: Embracing a Financially Empowered Future

The journey to financial freedom is a captivating expedition, one that can transform your life in profound ways. This voyage is not an elusive dream but a tangible reality, made attainable through a combination of discipline, strategic planning, and intelligent choices. In this comprehensive guide, tailored especially for beginners, we offer a detailed map to navigate the intricate landscape of personal finance. Let's delve into the key takeaways, each illuminating a crucial aspect of your quest for financial independence.

Understanding the Foundation: Building Blocks of Prosperity

Disciplined Budgeting and Savings:

> Budgeting isn't just about tracking expenses; it's about gaining control over your financial destiny. It empowers you to allocate resources efficiently and channel them toward your aspirations.

The Safety Net of Emergency Funds:

> Crafting a robust financial safety net by creating an emergency fund is vital. This fund shields you from the unexpected, ensuring you won't need to resort to high-interest debt in times of crisis.

Investing and Wealth Growth: Nurturing Your Financial Garden

Diversification:

> In the realm of investments, diversification is the key to managing risk and optimizing returns. It involves spreading your investments across various asset classes like stocks, bonds, and real estate.

Tax-Efficient Investing:

Tax-efficient strategies can significantly impact your investment returns. By maximizing tax-advantaged accounts and managing your tax liabilities wisely, you can keep more of your hard-earned money working for you.

Retirement Planning:

The journey to financial freedom extends well into retirement. Creating a comprehensive retirement plan involves optimizing Social Security benefits, formulating a retirement income strategy, and managing your retirement accounts diligently.

Creating Passive Income: Streams of Prosperity

Passive Income Streams:

Building multiple passive income sources, such as investments, rental properties, or online businesses, can accelerate your path to financial freedom. These income sources offer financial stability and flexibility.

Risk Management:

Understanding and mitigating financial risks become paramount as you progress on your financial journey. This includes strategies to cope with market volatility and preparation for unforeseen emergencies.

Managing Debt and Credit: Navigating the Financial Maze

Debt Management:

Tackling and reducing debt effectively is crucial for maintaining financial health. Prioritizing high-interest debts and pursuing a debt reduction strategy is a step towards liberation.

Responsible Credit Card Usage:

Credit cards can be both a boon and a bane. Responsible usage can boost your credit score, a crucial factor in your financial future. Understanding credit scores and their influencing factors is pivotal.

Protection and Planning: Safeguarding Your Legacy

Insurance:

Protecting your financial security through various insurance types is pivotal in preparing for unforeseen events or losses.

Estate and Legacy Planning:

Crafting a comprehensive estate plan ensures your assets are managed and distributed according to your wishes while minimizing estate taxes. It's a means of leaving a lasting financial legacy.

Advanced Strategies: Navigating the Complex Terrain

Tax Optimization:

Advanced strategies often involve intricate tax planning. These encompass tax-efficient investing and methods to minimize estate taxes, ensuring your wealth continues to grow efficiently.

Entrepreneurship and Business Ventures:

Exploring entrepreneurship or investing in startups can be avenues for wealth creation. These opportunities can amplify your financial success.

Passive Income:

Building passive income sources and exploring diverse investment opportunities can expedite your journey to financial freedom, enhancing your financial security.

In the grand tapestry of your financial life, these key takeaways are but the initial strokes of a masterpiece. Financial freedom is not a uniform destination; it's a personalized voyage. You embark on your unique path towards financial independence through these principles and actionable insights. This journey unlocks the potential for boundless abundance in your life, a reality waiting to be realized. Welcome to the exhilarating adventure of financial liberation.

About the Author

Samuel Wealthfield is a financial strategist, investment enthusiast, and author dedicated to empowering individuals on their journey to financial independence. With over two decades of experience in the finance industry, Oliver has honed his expertise in personal finance, wealth management, and investment strategies.

His passion for demystifying the complexities of finance led him to write his acclaimed book, "Unlocking Wealth: Your Blueprint to Financial Freedom and Prosperity." Through his writing, Oliver shares practical insights, actionable advice, and time-tested principles that empower readers, especially beginners, to take control of their financial destinies.

When he's not immersed in the world of finance, Oliver enjoys outdoor adventures, mentoring aspiring entrepreneurs, and spending quality time with his family. His mission is to inspire and guide individuals toward financial prosperity, one informed decision at a time.